THE PROCESS OF
HISTORICAL INQUIRY

THE PROCESS OF HISTORICAL INQUIRY

Everyday Lives of Working Americans

Jerome M. Clubb
Erik W. Austin
Gordon W. Kirk, Jr.

COLUMBIA UNIVERSITY PRESS
New York

COLUMBIA UNIVERSITY PRESS
NEW YORK   GUILDFORD, SURREY
Copyright © 1989 Columbia University Press

Library of Congress Cataloging-in-Publication Data

Clubb, Jerome M., 1928–
The process of historical inquiry : everyday lives of working Americans /
Jerome M. Clubb, Erik W. Austin, Gordon W. Kirk, Jr.
p.   cm.
Includes bibliographical references.
ISBN 0-231-06966-9 (alk. paper).—ISBN 0-231-06967-7 (pbk. :
alk. paper)
1. Working class—United States—History—19th century.
I. Austin, Erik W.   II. Kirk, Gordon W.   III. Title.
HD8072.C55   1989
305.5′62′097309034—dc20   89-23947
CIP

Casebound editions of Columbia University Press books are Smyth-sewn and printed on
permanent and durable acid-free paper.

Printed in the United States of America

c 10 9 8 7 6 5 4 3 2 1
p 10 9 8 7 6 5 4 3 2 1

CONTENTS

ACKNOWLEDGMENTS

Acknowledgments are inevitably expressions of both gratitude and apology. Upon finishing a project, no one can avoid recognizing that it has benefited from many contributions. At the same time, no one can fail to see shortcomings of the final product and ponder why—given the assistance of so many individuals and groups—that product is no better. Our effort here is not an exception. We have benefited from the assistance of many, but we can also now see ways in which the book could have been improved. Unfortunately, in writing books as in most other areas of life, human hindsight works a great deal better than foresight.

We cannot list all of the individuals who have assisted us in one way or the other in the preparation of this volume. To do so would be to attempt to list all of the people from whom we have learned and all of the situations from which we have gained experience. That we cannot provide such a list in no way lessens our gratitude. We can, however, express our gratitude to a number of individuals who assisted us in specific ways, in some instances without being conscious that they were doing so.

First on the list are students. Earlier versions of this book were used in manuscript form in over a dozen classes at the University of Michigan, Southern Illinois University, and Western Illinois University. We are grateful to the many students who patiently endured these earlier and highly imperfect versions. We have benefited from their many explicit suggestions and criticisms. We have particularly attempted to heed their silent criticisms, which came in the form of ill-concealed amazement that anyone could state things as badly as we often did, and their astonished disbelief that anyone could actually believe that some of our most cherished points were interesting, important and worthy of the time of serious students. We hope that we have rectified shortcomings that these students helped identify and that their discomfort in using earlier versions will contribute to reduction of the discomfort of students who will use the volume in the future.

A number of other individuals also contributed to the volume in direct ways. Ruth Wasem participated at the beginning of the effort that led to the volume. She carried out much of the early data analysis and contributed in a variety of other ways. Necessarily she went on to other things and could not continue in an effort that went on far too many years. Even so, the volume still reflects her efforts and we are grateful to her.

Much of the final most intricate data management and analysis for the volume was carried out by Peter Granda. We are grateful for his care and innovate effort. We are also grateful for Zack Allen's yeoman work in converting the tables and figures to publishable form. Donna Gotts was responsible for converting the many drafts through which the manuscript passed to readable form. We appreciate both her patience and tolerance and her excellent work.

We have also benefited from the comments and suggestions of a number of friends and colleagues. William H. Flanigan, Nancy Zingale, Howard W. Allen, James Q. Graham, and Patrick Horan read all or parts of earlier drafts. John Modell and Eric Monkkonen read an early version in its entirety and provided extensive written criticisms. We are also grateful for extended criticisms provided by two anonymous reviewers. We profited from all of these many comments and criticisms. We could not, however, follow all of the suggestions that we received. In some cases, to do so was beyond our capacity; in others, we persisted mulishly in the view that our own approach was superior. We cannot blame our critics for trying even though we sometimes resisted their advice. Because of their advice and assistance this is a much better book than it would otherwise be. We alone, of course, are responsible for its imperfections.

We must also express our gratitude to the Inter-university Consortium for Political and Social Research for providing the basic data on which the book is based. Although we could not have written the book without the Consortium, that organization bears no responsibility for our use of the data or for our interpretations. The basic data are available from the Consortium. As a consequence, anyone who wishes to do so can obtain the data and contest or extend our analyses and interpretations.

THE PROCESS OF
HISTORICAL INQUIRY

INTRODUCTION

This book is concerned with the social history of the United States in the latter nineteenth century. More specifically, we are concerned with the lives of industrial workers and their families in these years. Our primary attention is directed to one group of industrial workers and their families who lived and worked in the United States during the 1880s and the 1890s. We examine this group in some detail and at various points compare and contrast them with other groups that lived at the same or other times. Our goal is to gain improved understanding of the nature of society and the economy, of living and working conditions, and of family practices at the close of the nineteenth century. In this way, we can also gain a better understanding of the ways in which life in our own time differs from life in earlier years.

The book is concerned with the ordinary people of the times. Our use of the word "ordinary" should not be taken to mean that these people were uninteresting, or unimportant, but simply that these were not people of wealth, power, or position. They were much more like the great majority of Americans who lived and worked at the time than they were like the relatively small number of people who were wealthy or well to do, who held positions of importance, and who exercised power over other people.

Historical studies tend to focus disproportionately upon the few of affluence and position, and, indeed, history is often written from the perspective of such individuals. Only in recent years have growing numbers of historians and other social scientists begun to carry out systematic research into the living conditions, ways of life, and practices of the more ordinary people of the past.

These concerns are of considerable importance. It is only through such investigations that we can come to understand the actual conditions of life in the past. Such investigations provide a means to understand the way in which the society and economy of the past actually functioned, to comprehend the manner and degree to which different groups of individuals benefited (or failed to benefit) from the society and the economy, and to grasp the meaning and impact of social and economic change.

Without such investigations we could imagine, without justification, a lost "golden age" in which life was somehow happier and better than it is today. Conversely, without investigations of this sort we might see history, again without reason, as involving consistent and general "progress," with each generation enjoying better and happier conditions than the preceding generation. It is only through investigation of the lives of ordinary people, as well as the lives of other groups, that the facts of the case can be better established.

SOURCE MATERIAL

To address these issues, we employ data that were originally collected by the Office of the United States Commissioner of Labor from 1888 through 1890. The data were collected as a part of an investigation into the productivity of several industries in the United States and other countries. The investigation was mandated by an act of Congress in part out of concern for the impact of the protective tariff. As one element of the investigation, individuals in more than 8,000 families in the United States and other countries were interviewed. Members of these families were employed in the iron and steel, coal, glass, and woolen and cotton textile industries. The information collected through these interviews was then tabulated and published in the Annual Reports of the Commissioner of Labor for 1890 and 1891 under the titles *Costs of Production: Iron, Steel, Coal, Etc.* and *Costs of Production: The Textiles and Glass* (Washington, D.C.: Government Printing Office, 1891 and 1892).

For the purposes of our examination only the data for 3,043 families residing in the United States with members employed in the cotton and woolen textile industries are used. (The computer-readable version of the data employed here was obtained from the Inter-university Consortium for Political and Social Research in Ann Arbor, Michigan.) While the pages that follow focus primarily upon these families, inferences are made about other and larger groups of families. In a closing chapter, we discuss questions concerning the kinds of inferences about other groups that the data can and cannot support. Questions of this sort should, however, be kept clearly in mind as we proceed.

The source collection, as we will see, is both extensive and complicated. The data which it provides include the state in which the families resided and worked and the nationalities of the heads of the families. The specific occupations of the husbands in families are given along with the number, age, and sex of family members, whether family members were employed outside the household, and, in the case of children, whether they were in school or at home. The total income for the year is given for each family as is the income of working members and income obtained by the families from other sources. Extensive information bearing upon family expenditures is provided including the amounts spent on food (and particular types of food), the amounts spent for rent, clothing, fuel, recreation, books and newspapers, and various other purposes. Finally, the collection includes very brief descriptions of the households provided by the interviewers. (Figure 1 presents some examples of these interviewers' "remarks.")

The families themselves were highly diverse. All told, they resided in nineteen different states. The distribution of the families in terms of state of residence is given in table 1. As we can see, they were not evenly distributed among these states. Most of the families resided in the New England and Middle Atlantic states. More than 2,000 of the families, approximately 72 percent of the total, resided in these regions while fewer than a thousand, less than 28 percent of the total, resided in the South and the Border states.

The families were also diverse in nationality. Some twenty different national groups are represented in the data. Here again, however, these national groups are not equally represented. As table 2 indicates, over 1,500 of the families, more than 50 percent of the total, reported their nationality as "American." The other national groups were considerably smaller. The Irish constituted the next largest group after the Americans with 468 families. The other relatively large national groups were English, French Canadians, and Germans. Other national groups included only a small number of families.

Since the families are classified in terms of nationality, we can address questions concerning differences in the living conditions and family practices of various national groups. On the other hand, the nationality classification poses several problems that illustrate the complexity of the source collection. The collection gives only the nationalities of the heads of the families, in most cases the husbands. The nationalities of wives and children are not given. The meaning of nationality as used to classify the families is also unclear. We do not know whether the nationality given indicates the nation in which the individual was born or whether individuals were in fact born in the United States but described themselves as being of foreign descent, as some native-born individuals would today. We can employ the

PART III.—COST OF LIVING. 1207

TABLE XVII.—COTTON: COST OF LIVING, BY FAMILIES—Continued.

G.—REMARKS.

[No inference can be drawn from lack of fulness in some of these notes as uniformity of statement was found to be impracticable and was not insisted upon.]

1. Poor house; have a garden.
2. Good, neat home; have a garden and poultry.
3. House clean.
4. House well kept.
5. Wretched people, living in extreme poverty.
6. House neat and comfortable; have a garden, cow, and poultry.
7. Have a garden and poultry.
8. House poorly furnished.
9. Live in squalor.
10. Own property; man and wife drink.
11. Miserable house and miserable people.
12. Wretched house; surroundings filthy; have a sewing machine.
13. Poor house.
14. Fairly comfortable.
15. Surroundings plain and comfortless.
16. House plain, but comfortable; have a cow and poultry.
17. Fairly good house; disorderly; few comforts; have poultry.
18. Poor cabin; no comforts; have a small garden.
19. Good cottage; have a cow and poultry.
20. Good cottage; have a garden, cow, and poultry.
21. Good house; have a garden and two cows.
22. Wretched house.
23. Surroundings untidy; have a small garden.
24. Surroundings poor.
25. Company house; filthy; have an organ, cow, and poultry.
26. Miserable house; poor furniture; have a cow.
27. House poorly furnished; have a cow.
28. Company house; miserably furnished and dirty.
29. House poorly furnished; have a cow.
30. Miserable surroundings.
31. Tumble-down cottage; few comforts.
32. Poor cabin; have a small garden.
33. Have a garden and fruit trees, cow, hogs, and poultry.
34. Cabin with no door or windows; little furniture.
35. Cabin neat, but crowded; have a garden.
36. Poor house; little furniture; have a garden and cow.
37. Comfortable home; have a garden, cow, and poultry.
38. Poor house; scant furniture; have poultry.
39. Good cottage.
40. No comforts.
42. Comfortable and tasteful home; have a garden, cow, and poultry.
43. Have a cow.
44. House neat and comfortable; have carpets, and a sewing machine.
45. House neat and comfortable.
48. House plainly furnished; have carpets.
49. House neatly and comfortably furnished.
50. House neat and comfortable; have carpets, organ, and sewing machine.
51. House neat and comfortable; have carpets.
53. House poorly furnished.
54. Comfortable tenement.
59. House neat and comfortable.
62. House poorly furnished.
63. House poorly furnished; own a farm.
64. House comfortably furnished.
65. Good tenement; poorly furnished.
66. House poorly furnished; have carpets and a piano.
67. House poorly furnished; have carpets.
68. House poorly furnished; have carpets; deficit caused by sickness.
69. House poorly furnished; have one carpet and a sewing machine.
70. House plainly furnished.
71. House comfortable; have carpets; deficit caused by sickness.
72. House plainly furnished.
73. House comfortably furnished.
74. House poorly furnished.
75. House plainly furnished; have carpets.
76. House comfortably furnished; have an organ; own property.
77. House poorly furnished; have carpets.
78. House plainly furnished; have carpets.
79. House poorly furnished; have carpets and a melodeon.
81. House fairly well furnished.
82. House poorly furnished.
83. Good tenement; poorly furnished.
89. House poorly furnished.
90. House poorly furnished.
92. House poorly furnished.
95. House poorly furnished.
97. Good house; plainly furnished.
98. House plainly furnished.
99. House out of repair; poorly furnished; have a sewing machine.
100. House in good order; plainly furnished; have a sewing machine.

Interviewer's "remarks" contained in original source collection. SOURCE: *Seventh Annual Report of the Commissioner of Labor, 1891*. Cost of Production: The Textiles and Glass. Volume 2(part 3)—Cost of Living (Washington, D.C.: U.S. Government Printing Office, 1892), p. 107.

nationalities given in the data in examining the families, but we do not know the precise meaning of these classifications.

The small number of families in some nationality groups also poses a difficulty as does the small representation of some states. We can recognize that some of the state and national groups are too small to be examined independently. We can also suspect that some of these small groups were unusual in at least some respects and present a potential source of distortion. For these reasons we must combine state and national groups in various ways for purposes of examination and analysis. At some points we must also exclude groups from particular applications in order to avoid potentially misleading findings.

The data collection is also marked by other limitations of a more general nature. The sources do not give us a full explanation of how the families

Table 1
State of Residence of Families with Workers
Employed in the Cotton and Woolen Industries

States	No. of Families
New England States	
Connecticut	296
Maine	275
Massachusetts	418
New Hampshire	155
Rhode Island	95
	1,239
Middle Atlantic States	
Delaware	48
New Jersey	85
New York	401
Pennsylvania	426
	960
Southern States	
Virginia	124
Alabama	43
Georgia	199
Louisiana	10
Mississippi	34
North Carolina	148
South Carolina	33
	591
Border States	
Kentucky	20
Maryland	164
Tennessee	69
	253
All Families	3,043

were selected. We have little information as to how the interviews were conducted and copies of the interview questionnaire have not been found. There is every indication that great care was taken by officials of the Commissioner's office in collecting and tabulating the data. Even so there can be little doubt that the data are marked by errors introduced by the original interviewers while tabulating the data, during the publication process, or during the present-day process of converting the data to computer-readable form. Some of these are noted in the text that follows, and it is undoubtedly the case that still other errors exist that have not been detected.

We must keep limitations such as these clearly in mind when using the data and in evaluating inferences based on them. Questions to be constantly asked concern the inferences that can or cannot be supported by the data and the questions that can or cannot be meaningfully addressed. While we must keep these problems and limitations in mind, we should not regard them as disabling. They are no more than illustrations of the kinds of problems and limitations that mark all historical sources and with which all historians must always contend. It will also be clear that despite such limitations, the data collection is a remarkably rich and fascinating historical source that provides a glimpse into a very rare detail of life at a distant historical time.

Table 2
Nationality of Heads of Families

Nationality	Number of Families
United States	1,561
French Canada	226
Canada	98
England	353
Ireland	468
Scotland	81
Wales	26
France	36
Switzerland	3
Portugal	5
Germany	160
Poland	1
Austria	6
Hungary	1
Bohemia	2
Italy	2
Russia	1
Sweden	10
Norway	1
Denmark	2
All Families	**3,043**

QUESTIONS AND EXPECTATIONS

In the following pages the data collection is used to address a variety of substantive historical questions. In many cases it is also possible to formulate, at least in general ways, the expected answers to these questions. Generalizations are at hand in the writings of contemporary observers, historians, and other scholars that bear upon questions of concern. These generalizations suggest hypotheses which we test in the following pages. A part of the task in our examination, in short, is to test, refine, refute, confirm, modify, or extend generalizations about the history of the nation. It is useful at this point to formulate some of these questions and hypotheses. In general, such a formulation will prove useful in asking questions and designing analysis strategies to answer them. The expected results from application of those strategies are also set forth.

One broad set of hypotheses concerns the income and living conditions of foreign- or immigrant-stock families as compared with those of the native stock. Foreign stock and immigrant stock are interchangeable terms that were conventionally used in these years to describe people who were either born in other countries or whose parents were born in other countries. We will so use the terms here. The term native stock was applied to people who were born in the United States and whose parents were also born in the United States. We will also use the term in that sense. In very general terms, we would expect that foreign-stock families and individuals would tend to have lower incomes and be less well off than those of native stock.

These are several reasons to expect differences. The various national groups that migrated to the United States in the nineteenth century differed in many ways from each other and from the native stock. English was not the native language of some groups, and the national groups also differed in educational levels, skills, and experiences. Some groups belonged to religions and had cultural characteristics that were not fully acceptable either to other foreign-stock groups or to the native stock. Because of such differences some foreign-stock groups were better equipped to exist in an English-speaking world than others; some were better equipped in terms of education, skills, and experience to compete for better-paying jobs; and some groups undoubtedly encountered discrimination in that competition.

While these considerations all underlie our expectation that the foreign-stock families tended to be less well off than the native stock, they also suggest ways in which our expectations must be qualified and refined. Obviously, there were differences between the various specific foreign-stock groups, and some groups undoubtedly were better off than others. We may even find that families and individuals of some nationalities were better off than some native-stock groups. What we need, then, is a formulation of more complicated expectations with respect to the income and conditions of specific foreign and native-stock groups.

During these years, the states and regions of the nation also differed widely in economic conditions, employment opportunities, and the like. Thus one set of hypotheses concerns variations in income levels and living conditions between states and regions. For several reasons we would expect to find that income levels and living conditions were worse in the Southern states than elsewhere in the United States. The South was not as heavily industrialized as many of the states of the North. It was also the case that the Southern states still felt in the 1880s and 1890s the debilitating effects of Civil War and Reconstruction.

And there was the fact of racial discrimination. Through discriminatory practices, the income levels and working conditions of blacks were suppressed. These practices also worked to depress the income levels and working and living conditions of whites. For these reasons we would expect to find that the income levels and conditions of many Southern families were worse than those of families in other regions.

Further questions concern family size, structure, and practices. Here again, differences among nationality and, perhaps, regional groups might be expected. We would expect that some nationality groups had larger numbers of children than families of other nationalities. There is evidence that among some groups children tended to remain at home until an older age than among other groups. Given a little thought, we could formulate more precise hypotheses as to differences in these respects between specific nationality groups.

A variety of questions also arise concerning expenditure and consumption patterns. Basic questions concern how well people in the latter nineteenth century actually lived; what a given level of income would purchase and how good a standard of living it would support; what people chose to purchase; and how much choice they actually had in making such decisions. We would expect differences in expenditure and consumption patterns between nationality and regional groups. The data provide limited information bearing upon expenditures for religious purposes, reading materials, and intoxicants, so that variations between national and other groups in this regard might be expected.

Equally important questions have to do with the relationship between income levels, and expenditure patterns. A simple and obvious expectation would be that at higher levels of income larger amounts would be spent for discretionary purposes—in other words, for non-necessities. In this case, we might take the discretionary purposes for which income was actually spent as indications of values, tastes, and preferences. The converse and equally obvious expectation would be that at lower levels of income greater amounts were spent on necessities. In this case, we would take the actual choices made in spending as indications of the economies dictated by lower income levels and their impact upon living conditions.

These are, of course, rather broad and general questions. A variety of preliminary subquestions must be formulated and addressed in order to come to grips with these larger issues. What we need is a "chain" of questions, analytic strategies designed to address them, and expected results which cumulate to address these larger questions. And here we must recognize a sad fact: we cannot expect final, complete, certain, and definitive answers. We can increase our confidence in the accuracy of some of our generalizations and decrease our confidence in others, but certainty will elude us.

FINDINGS AND INFERENCES

We employ the data for the 3,043 families of textile workers to address these and related questions. The families are interesting in their own right, and statements and generalizations about them are intrinsically important. We also use these data and families to draw inferences about other groups of families and individuals that lived at the same or somewhat different times. We will often be able on the basis of data analysis to make statements and generalizations with reasonable confidence in their accuracy about the characteristics of these families and their members and about relationships between these characteristics. However, we will also confront questions of the degree to which statements and generalizations about these specific families and individuals also apply to other families and individuals. Put differently, the question is the degree and ways in which these specific families and individuals are representative of other families and individuals.

The issues here will become obvious if we shift the questions around a bit. How well do these families represent all families at the time with members employed in the cotton and woolen textile industries? How well do these families represent all families at the time with members employed in industries of whatever kind? How well do they represent all families at the time? Obviously, we would give different answers to each of these questions, and have differing levels of confidence in the representative quality of the data for different groups.

We know that in selecting the families to be interviewed the officials of the Commissioner's Office intended that the information so obtained would be representative of all families of workers employed in the cotton and

woolen textile industry. They intended, in other words, to employ a representative sample of the families of cotton and woolen textile workers. The
reports of the Commissioner of Labor concede limitations in this respect.
Some families that were approached refused to be interviewed, and some
were unable to provide the required information. There is also some indication that the permission of employers was required as a condition for
interviewing the families. If that was the case, and we are not certain that it
was, we might ask in what degree and in what way this requirement
rendered the sample of families less representative.

While it is clear that the data collection was intended to be representative of the families of cotton and woolen textile workers, we are virtually
certain that the set of 3,043 families does not constitute a *probability* sample
of the sort employed in modern-day sample surveys and polls. Samples of
this sort involve selection of a small group (sample) from a larger population—as the population of the nation, a state, or of another group defined
in some other fashion—that is statistically representative of the larger
population. Because of the way in which such samples are selected they are
representative of the larger populations within a known probable margin of
error. As a consequence, if particular characteristics or relationships are
observed in a statistical sample, it can be inferred with a known probability
of error that the same characteristic or relationship is also present in the
larger population from which the sample was selected. Statistical sampling
procedures of this sort were not known in the late 1880s. Thus the present
data cannot be seen as a statistical sample.

The fact that the sample of 3,043 families employed here is not a statistical sample in the modern sense of the word does not mean that we can
make no inferences on the basis of the data to other and larger groups of
families and individuals. It does mean that we must exercise considerable
care in drawing such inferences and that possible limitations of such inferences must be taken into account.

It will be clear as well that the degree of confidence in the representative
quality of these data will depend upon the questions we address. For the
purposes of some questions we can have greater confidence in the data than
for other questions: We can surmise, for example, that the data provide a
reliable means to assess the standards of living that could be supported by
families in different areas at different levels of income. Other questions of
this sort will come to mind for which confidence in the representative
quality of the data would be relatively high. Even this example, however,
suggests qualifications; a farming family that grew some or all of its own food
could maintain a better standard of living at a given income level than could
an urban family at the same income level that grew none of its own food.
The point is, of course, that care must be taken in formulating questions

and in assessing the utility and limitations of the data collection as a means to address them.

METHODS AND APPROACHES

The pages that follow may seem unusual in several respects. Each of the chapters that follow is concerned with substantive historical issues and questions. The reader is invited to join directly in the process of exploring these issues and devising solutions to the historical questions considered. In other words the reader is invited to gain experience in the ways historians actually work and conduct research. To do so the characteristics and limitations of historical source material must be recognized. At various points, therefore, we discuss problems of error and other limitations of source materials, their possible consequences, and means by which we can sometimes compensate for error and other limitations of our sources.

In exploring the historical issues and questions of concern we must use a few simple tools of quantitative analysis. These tools should not be troublesome nor should they be a distraction from the substantive issues of concern. If these tools are already familiar, the reader should simply pass over the paragraphs that explain them and examine only their specific applications and the inferences drawn on the basis of those applications.

These tools are employed in the text and their use is suggested as a means to address particular historical questions. It will be clear, of course, that this book is not intended as a text in quantitative methods. We introduce, describe, and treat these tools in nontechnical terms. Our effort is only to provide a basis for a conceptual understanding of them, so that they can be used in addressing substantive issues. We hope, however, that their use will prove sufficiently interesting and that their value for historical inquiry and for numerous other purposes will be sufficiently apparent that some readers will wish to acquire formal training in their use.

In writing the following pages a central goal has been to make explicit the process of inference and the assumptions that underlie the formulation of particular historical questions and the design of analytic strategies to address them. In some cases this approach also involves false starts and leads into blind alleys. As it happens, false starts and blind alleys are an unavoidable part of the game. The effort here is to allow the reader to follow the inferential process and to recognize assumptions. In this way the frailties of that process and the weaknesses of assumptions can be noted and the limitations, shortcomings, and contingent nature of resulting conclusions and generalizations can be recognized.

Some readers will be troubled by the sense of uncertainty conveyed by such words as assumption and inference. In fact assumptions and inferences are also tools. They are necessary tools, and we cannot proceed without them. Their use does involve elements of uncertainty. Here we must return to an earlier point. Uncertainty is unavoidable in all inquiry and seems to be a consistent characteristic of what we call knowledge.

— 1 —
WORKING AND
LIVING CONDITIONS

To start, let us briefly inventory some of the information that is already available about the families of concern here. Clearly, we already know a great deal about these families, and still more information can reasonably be inferred; even more is readily at hand. Indeed, much of what we already know or can reasonably assume is so obvious that it could easily be overlooked. So let us give some thought to what is already known.

THE HISTORICAL CONTEXT

The historical context in which the families lived is a source of substantial information. The latter nineteenth century was a time of continuing and rapid industrialization, during which the proportion of the national labor force employed in agricultural pursuits was steadily and rapidly declining while the proportion employed in industry and manufacturing was increasing. The process of industrialization included several concomitant elements of relevance to an understanding of the conditions and experiences of these families and of other families like them. One such element was the process of mechanization, the substitution of mechanical power for human and animal power and the replacement of "by hand" processes in industry and manufacturing by mechanical ones.

Mechanization was already far advanced in the latter nineteenth century. Work in mills and factories increasingly involved tending machines—and machines of steadily growing size—that did the work of producing commodities. To an ever-growing degree, workers themselves were no longer producing commodities manually. Mechanization also tended to reduce the skills required of individual workers. It meant that workers were increasingly employed in limited and specialized tasks and did not see the task of producing a particular commodity through from start to finish. One implication was that workers tended to become more nearly substitutable "interchangeable parts."

Another element of industrialization was growth in the size of industrial and manufacturing establishments. While small firms and establishments did not disappear, larger ones, which employed large numbers of workers, became more common. Smaller enterprises, in which owners sometimes worked side by side with employees, tended to become less common. Use of machines permitted, and required, employment of larger numbers of workers and also required large investments of capital. Hence realization of the "economies of scale" permitted by mechanization dictated larger rather than smaller firms and factories. While the processes of industrialization and mechanization created demand for labor, they also worked to increase the distance and the disparity of power between owners and managers on the one hand, and workers on the other.

Industrialization was accompanied by change in the nature of markets for commodities. As industrial and manufacturing firms now often produced for a national and, indeed, international market rather than for a local one, they became subject to competition from distant firms for distant markets and to fluctuations in national and international demand for commodities. Since periods of oversupply or reduced demand dictated reduction of production, individual workers found that demand for their services would fluctuate. The consequences were periodic unemployment and loss of income through plant closures and layoffs.

Another aspect of the period was the prevailing economic and business theories and ideologies. The labor of individual workers was often seen as a commodity in the same sense as a bolt of cloth or another manufactured item. Wages and employment were seen as subject to the "laws of supply and demand" and were expected to fluctuate as the scarcity or abundance of workers with required skills, and the need for them, fluctuated. Governmental unemployment and relief programs were rare or nonexistent as were regulations governing the conditions of labor. As a consequence, workers were usually left to their own resources in the event of layoffs or unemployment and in coping with working conditions. Some firms, particularly larger firms, did maintain private programs that provided various worker benefits and, more rarely, a measure of security against unemployment. In some cases, these programs were motivated as much by interest in maintaining an orderly and disciplined labor force and to prevent unionization as they were by interest in the well-being of employees.

Urbanization was a related development of the period. These years were marked by rapid growth of cities and towns as the balance of population shifted from the countryside and rural areas to the towns and cities. One source of urban growth was immigration. While immigration, of course, had been a continuing fact of life from the beginning of the nation, the influx of immigrants—particularly from southern and eastern Europe at the end of the nineteenth and in the early twentieth centuries—was unparalleled in the history of the nation.

For many of the towns and cities of the time, these developments led to a variety of pressing problems. Sanitation facilities and instrumentalities to maintain law, order, and public safety became inadequate. Schools, parks, and playgrounds—to the degree they existed—were similarly inadequate. Housing scarcities developed with the consequence of crowding and sub-standard living conditions, particularly for the very poor and for lower income groups in general.

It can be readily surmised that all of this influenced the lives and working conditions of the families of concern here and of other families like them. Obviously, the heads of these families worked in the cotton and woolen textile industry and it is highly likely that many of the wives and children who worked outside the home were also employed in textile mills and factories. The textile industry was one of the leading industries of the time and was marked by many of the characteristics sketched above. It cannot be imagined that all of the working members of these families toiled in large and impersonal mills and factories, but it can be surmised that many did. Similarly, not all of these families lived in large cities or towns; but some of them did, and they experienced the urban problems and difficulties of the period.

Most of the working members of the families were manual laborers of one skill level or another. It is virtually certain that many of them worked under hazardous conditions. They used machinery—looms, carding machines, and the like—that had few safety devices. Thus they faced the risk of injury and loss of limbs. Working conditions presented other hazards as well. There was often dust and lint in the air of the workplace so that there was a risk of various respiratory disorders. A measure of insecurity and financial uncertainty was a fact of life among the families. Like other industrial workers of the time they sometimes faced layoffs and plant closures that often came without warning.

Certainly, these people were poorly educated by our standards, and probably even by the standards of their own times; certainly they were not wealthy. Whether we want to call them "poor people," however, is another matter. It is probable that the large majority of the families ranked somewhere in the lower third of the income distribution of the nation. That is, two-thirds of the families of the nation probably had larger incomes than the majority of these families. To speak in terms of social class, it would be sensible to think of these people as working class or at most lower middle class.

On the other hand, these families were probably not among the nation's poorest. As was seen in table 2 of the Introduction, a substantial number of the families were of foreign stock. As was also seen in the table, however, most of the foreign-stock families were of Canadian or western and northern European nationalities. Only a relatively small number were from southern or eastern Europe. In other words, these families were not part of the "new" immigration that brought large numbers of people from southern and eastern European countries to the United States during the latter nineteenth and the early twentieth centuries. It was these latter groups that tended to constitute the largest segment of the urban poor rather than the "older" immigrant stock from northern and western Europe. Thus it can be suspected that the families of concern here were relatively better off than many other families and particularly the newer immigrants.

FAMILY CONDITIONS AND CHARACTERISTICS

The generalizations sketched above suggest broad expectations about the families and their living and working conditions. We also need, however, a more detailed view in order to refine and confirm or disconfirm these broad expectations. One clue to the kinds of people these were and to the way they lived is provided by a letter written by a women interviewed by an agent of the Commissioner of Labor and published in one of the Department's reports.[1] The letter provides highly personal and human insights as well as, if read closely, useful assistance in interpreting findings that will be presented below.

  Dear Sir:

  In pursuance of the question of living and what it costs, the amount of money the bread winner received for his labor, and the mincing it takes to make it "sufficient unto the day," I offer you the result of my investigation at home, which I believe to be a correct statement of our expenses for one year:

White flour	600 pounds, at	$ 0.03 per pound	$18.00
Graham flour	150 pounds, at	.035 per pound	4.80
"A" sugar	156 pounds, at	.08 per pound	$18.00
Coffee			
(roasted)	52 pounds at	.30 per pound	15.60
Fresh meat	546 pounds, at	.10 per pound	54.60

Salt meat	156 pounds, at	.125 per pound	19.50
Baking powder	12 pounds, at	.50 per pound	6.00
Tea	6 pounds, at	.75 per pound	4.50
Beans	60 pounds, at	.05 per pound	3.00
Butter	104 pounds, at	.20 per pound	20.80
Lard	100 pounds, at	.10 per pound	10.00
Salt	60 pounds, at	.01 per pound	.60
Pepper	1.25 pounds, at	.35 per pound	.44
Soap	96 pounds, at	.05 per pound	4.80
Starch	12 pounds, at	.10 per pound	1.20
Potatoes	18 bushels, at	1.40 per bushel	25.20
Onions	3 bushels, at	1.60 per bushel	4.80
Coal Oil	52 gallons, at	.15 per gallon	7.80
Vinegar	4 gallons, at	.20 per gallon	.80
Eggs	24 dozen, at	.15 per dozen	3.60
Yeast	1 dozen pkgs., at	.05 per package	.60
Matches	1 dozen boxes, at	.025 per box	.30
Bluing	4 bottles, at	.05 per bottle	.20
Brooms	4, at	.25 per broom	1.00

Total grocery account	$220.62
House rent, $7 per month	84.00
Fuel, $2 per ton	24.00
Shoes (4 pairs at $3; 6 pairs at $1.50; 6 pairs at $1)	27.00
Barbering (hair cutting once a month, at 25 cents; shaving once a week at 10 cents, and twice a week half the time, with an occasional shampoo)	10.00
Tobacco (a 5-cent package and 2 cigars a week)	7.80
Reading (a daily paper at 10 cents a week and a Sunday paper at 5 cents)	7.80
Total	81.22
Wages (average $48 per month)	576.00
Expenses	381.22
Surplus	$194.78

Number in family, 7; number of children, 4; ages 2, 4, 6, and 7 years.

The management that "maintains a six-dollar house on four dollars" will not conform to statistics; hence I must explain that I save four pounds a week of white flour by using graham, and that the flour, lard, baking powder, and sugar on my list are sufficient, if we keep light bread most of the time, and make the pies and cakes few and very far between. I use "A" sugar because there is less shrinkage than in other brands. I make fresh coffee once a day. Butter and eggs are more frequently used as substitutes for meat than otherwise. Crackers, milk, rice, wheat, cheese, pickles, and spices are substitutes for articles of kindred value. All prepared meats, prepared and tropical fruits are bits of extravagance in which we may indulge to the cost of something more indispensable.

The fitness of things must largely control, not the bill of fare alone, but the purchase. In summer and winter alike I must try to buy the food that will sustain us the greatest number of meals at the lowest price, and I should like to shake hands with the person who can reduce it to figures. The cost of pounds, bushels, gallons, etc., on my list are computed at what they actually cost me now. Could I buy in larger quantities, I could render a different account. The dividing-up process is the real business of the working man (or his wife). The families are not few who do just as I did a few weeks ago, when I found on Monday morning that I had just $3.35 with which to feed seven of us until Saturday night, and keep the house going. Indeed, some do better figuring than I did, for I, fortunately, had both fuel and flour. At our house meat is the basis, and in an emergency like this we use the coarser meats. So I arranged to have fresh meat once a day. I bought a dime's worth of flank steak twice, at 6.25 cents per pound, a soup bone at 10 cents, a 15-cent "boil" at 8 cents per pound, a 15-cent roast at 10 cents per pound, and two pounds of bacon, all of which cost me 85 cents. Then I bought as follows: Sugar, 25 cents; tea, 10; coffee, 30; baking powder, 15; soap, 10; coal oil, 15; cabbage, 10, potatoes, 35; pickles, 10; onions, 10; dried peaches, 15; crackers, 10; beans, 10; eggs, 15; and butter, 20. I have been asked, "Why buy pickles and onions when the same amount of money would buy rice and wheat, which surely is cheaper, because so wholesome?" My experience with my children is that rice and wheat require butter or sugar, or both, to make them palatable, and as butter and sugar are luxuries with us we must use them sparingly. With a dime's worth of onions, a peck of potatoes will last us a week, at a cost of 45 cents. Without them a half bushel of potatoes are used, at 65 cents, a difference, you see, of enough money to buy beefsteak twice. As for pickles, a dozen at a cost of 10 cents will last us a week, and make salt meat endurable, and they last longer than a peck of apples at 25 or 30 cents a peck. If you wish a demonstration of this fact, just place a peck of apples, no matter how hard and green, where 4 or 5 children have access to them. In addition to all this why and wherewith a visitor adds to the expense $2 per week, and the living is no better than before. This, I think, is due to the disadvantage of buying in small quantities. If I count the cost for a single meal, no more than 5 cents extra for meat, and the same for vegetables (the smallest quantity I could buy), the cost in one week is $2.10. Two visitors a single meal, at different times, cost more than both at the same meal.

Ordinarily our expenses (groceries, fuel and rent) are from $6 to $7 per week. In the course of a year we have $194.78 with which to buy clothing and household incidentals. Now these "clothing and incidental" items are a host within themselves. Divide $194.78 among seven persons for clothing alone, and we have but $2.32 a month. The "incidentals" are interminable. Stamps, writing material, thread, needles, buttons, pins, lamp flues; in fact everything, from car fare uptown on a rainy day, and a bottle of Castoria for the baby, to ammonia and carpet tacks during house cleaning. Could we use a year's earnings as I have divided them we might get through, but bills that were made when the children were sick or the husband out of employment the year previous press heavily sometimes, and cut into the present year's earnings. Or if the factory shuts down without warning, as it did last year for six weeks, we have a growing expense with nothing to counterbalance. An itemized account of the expenditures of the $194.78, compared with an itemized account of what we must and do have on credit I suppose will reveal the frustration of our efforts. I think sometimes in our efforts to make both ends meet we are like a kitten I once had who tried with all his little might to catch his tail. He kept twirling round and round and round, always with the end he so much wanted in view, but never quite catching it.

No doubt this "affair" needs boiling down; things I write usually do; but the man who serves the people with a dish of facts can do that to suit himself.

Yours, socially,
Mrs. J.E.B.

If it is assumed that the letter is authentic—and there is no obvious reason to assume otherwise—what can we say about the woman and her family? Clearly she appears to have been literate and highly articulate, although it is likely that the letter was edited and corrected before it was published in the report. If the letter is taken at face value, she was—and needed to be—a good manager.

But what kind of life does she describe? Does she describe a life of poverty? It is clear that the members of this family did not have all they wanted; and they often did not have what they wanted—they often had to substitute things they liked less well for other things that they would have

preferred. And there are signs of stringencies. Apparently unemployment
and sickness were sometimes experienced. This woman was not always able
to buy in large quantities. As a consequence, she was unable to capitalize
on bargains and was forced to pay higher prices than would have otherwise
been necessary. One reason for not buying in larger quantities may have
been the absence of refrigeration and other food preservation facilities. But
the letter can also be taken as suggesting that weekly income was simply
not sufficient to allow buying in large quantities.

There are these and other indications of stringency and perhaps poverty.
On the other hand, there is no indication that the family was starving or
that they suffered from malnutrition. (It is the case, however, that the diets
of both poor and well-to-do people of these times often tended to be
deficient in terms of what is now recognized as necessary for good health
and child development. Thus many people, almost regardless of income,
suffered from some form of malnutrition.) There is no indication that the
family lacked heat, shelter and basic clothing, and there are indications of a
few small luxuries. They were able to have guests for meals at least occasionally, the husband was sometimes shaved by a barber, there were shampoos
at the barber shop, and there was tobacco, even an occasional cigar.

Our difficulty in deciding whether or not to describe this family as poor,
and whether or not to call certain expenditures luxuries, is in part because
notions like poverty and luxury are examples of relative concepts. Going to
the barber or using tobacco might not be thought of as luxuries, or at least
not as very big ones. They are, however, examples of things that the family
could have survived without, although life would have been less pleasant.
The family was poor in comparison with the way many of us live. It is by no
means certain that the family was poor in comparison with other families of
the time and there is no indication that they thought of themselves as poor.

What this means is that in order to classify people as poor or things as
luxuries, some standard of comparison is necessary. Some more or less
arbitrary standard could be used, as is sometimes done. It could simply be
said that below some level of income, or if money is insufficient to buy
certain things in certain amounts, people will be classified as poor. Such a
standard need not, of course, be completely arbitrary. It might be set, for
example, in terms of the minimum income required to provide an adequate
diet, clothing, and shelter. But even here we would encounter difficulties
and disagreement in defining "adequate."

This presents another difficulty encountered in working with historical
source materials—one that can be illustrated by posing additional questions
and attempting to answer them by examining the content of the letter.
What was this woman's mood? What can be said about her morale and
attitude toward life and her own situation? After reading the letter some

might answer that her mood was close to despair. Her life was hard; there was never enough; money would not stretch; there was no hope that conditions would improve for her, her husband, or their children; and there was an ever-present risk that through illness or unemployment living conditions would become worse. Others might give an opposite answer and describe her mood as one of pride and high morale. Yes, life was hard and it was difficult to make the money stretch, but she was managing. She was doing well by her husband and children, and she knew it; she would continue to do well by them, and she was confident that she would be able to meet all problems as they arose in the future.

Obviously, the answer given to such questions depends in part on our personal experience and reflects our own assessment of what we would feel if we lived in similar circumstances. The point is, these are our interpretations of the letter. Our own reactions are being "read" into the letter and these reactions may not have been what the author of the letter felt or intended to convey. The fact is that the woman says nothing explicitly about her mood, her morale, or her attitude toward life. Our statements about her mood, her morale, and her attitudes are based in part upon the words she chose to use, the way she arranged them, and—above all—the way we think that we and others would feel if we found ourselves in circumstances similar to those she describes. Our statements may be interesting and plausible, but there is no direct evidence to support them.

This same problem will be encountered in even more severe ways when examining the larger data collection. We will be able to learn a great deal about the *objective* conditions of the families; it may prove tempting to make statements about the attitudes, mood, and morale of family members; and it would be interesting and useful to do so. But the data tell nothing about *subjective* moods and morale, and if such statements are made they will be made without concrete evidence to support them.

The letter also raises further questions concerning the degree to which the family described was typical or representative of other families included in the data collection. One approach to this question, and for some of us an interesting and even fascinating approach, would be to use the data to examine specific families and to ask whether and to what degree these other families were like the family described in the letter.

As an example, the data for Household 121 in the collection described a family of five living in Connecticut. The husband was of English nationality and worked as a loom fixer. The wife did not work outside the home, although undoubtedly she maintained the household, cooked meals, mended and perhaps made clothes, and contributed to the family income in these and many other ways. Husband and wife were in their middle years. There were three children, two boys (or young men) aged eighteen and sixteen and a girl (or young woman) aged fourteen. Two of the children were working and one was in school. It would probably be plausible to assume that it was the girl who was in school, but the data do not provide this information. The family's income, aside from the unmeasured contribution of the wife, came from three sources. The husband's income for the year was $493.50 (or 47.3 percent of the total family income), $524.50 (or 50.3 percent of the total) came from the children, and $25.00 (2.4 percent) came from other sources.

The data also provide a good bit of information about the way the family lived. A total of $377.87 (or 36.2 percent) of family income was reported as spent for food, including tea, coffee, and sugar. Their diet seems to have been reasonably high in protein content. The amounts of food products purchased are not consistently given and full information on food prices is not available, although the letter reproduced above does provide some information of this sort. At the time the price of beef ranged somewhere in the neighborhood of seven to fifteen cents per pound. Since the family in Household 121 reported spending $56.16 on beef, it can be assumed that somewhere in the neighborhood of 375 to 800 pounds of beef was consumed. These calculations could also be carried out for other food products and it would be possible to more fully reconstruct the consumption patterns of the family. It would then also be possible to compare the consumption patterns of this family with that of other families, with consumption patterns today, and with modern dietary requirements for good health.

Examination of the reported expenditures provides some surprises. The data indicate that the family consumed 472 pounds of sugar during the year, or an average of over four ounces of sugar per person in the family per day. In contrast, the family reported spending only $3.60 on vegetables (other than potatoes and rice) during the year. It is possible that these are errors. The amounts spent on these items may have been misreported, the interviewer may have misrecorded them; or they might be the result of typographical errors in publishing the data. On the other hand it might be recalled that canning was a common means of preserving foods and that in canning large amounts of sugar are often used. Thus the amount of sugar reported may be plausible.

The entire family income was not, of course, spent on food. A total of $481.65 (or 46.2 percent) was reported as spent on non-food items. Rent, heat and lighting were reported as costing the family $101.20 for the year, or 9.7 percent of total income. This is substantially below the share of income that a modern family of moderate means would spend for similar purposes, and this is also a comparison that could be made more precisely. A total of $135.75 (13 percent of family income) was reported as spent on clothing, $28.50 (2.7 percent) on furniture, and $14.00 (1.3 percent) on taxes and insurance. Again, these percentages are probably below the expenditures for similar purposes of families today, but we would want to make these comparisons more precisely and think carefully about the implications of the differences that would be observed.

Expenditures were also reported for what might be though of as non-necessities. These include expenditures for organizations, religion, charity, books and newspapers, and amusements and vacation which amount all told to $57.00, or 5.5 percent of total income. Whether or not we want to call these expenditures luxuries, they are examples of discretionary expenditures. These are things that the family could have lived without, although some of us might consider expenditures for religious purposes as hardly discretionary. If the matter is given some thought, we might suspect that some of the food expenditures were also discretionary—the family could have substituted other and cheaper commodities for some of those actually purchased.

This was clearly not a wealthy family, but it appears from the data to have been reasonably prosperous. Family income was sufficient to allow at least some discretionary spending, and the family ended the year with a surplus of $183.48 (17.6 percent of their total income) either to pay off past debts or to lay aside for the future. They did not own their own house, but they rented one with seven rooms and were apparently not excessively crowded. The interviewer commented "House neat and comfortable, has carpet in every room." The family undoubtedly ran the risks of unemployment, sickness, and injury that would have reduced income. At the time the family was able to enjoy at least a few of the good things of life, and we might conclude that this family tended to be better off than the family described in the letter.

Here again we must ask whether this family was typical or representative of other families. Again, for comparison, still other families might be described. A detailed description of Household 82 in the collection is presented in table 1.1. This family also lived in Connecticut and consisted of nine people, a husband of Canadian nationality, a wife, and seven children. Working as a laborer, the husband earned $350 during the year (66.7 percent of the total family income), while one working child earned an additional $175 (33.3 percent of total family income). The wife did not work outside the home. Three of the seven children were "at home" and one was "at work," while the "work-school-home" status of the remaining three children is reported as unknown. The economic situation of Household 82 was clearly less comfortable than that of Household 121. This family not only had more members to support, but also had to support them with an income that was only about half ($525) that of Family 121. Expenditures for food for the family was $437.54, or approximately 83 percent of total family

income. The family spent relatively little on non-food items ($196.57, or
37.4 percent of its total income). It was obviously much harder for Family
82 to make ends meet; in fact, the family ended the year with a deficit of
$109.11. The interviewer's comment confirms our suspicion that the living
standard was low: the comment merely states "House poorly furnished."

It is clear that the latter two families were rather strikingly different and
both differed from the family described in the letter. Although Household
121 had a standard of living well below that of many of us, it was much
better off than Household 82 and probably better off than the family described in the letter. Given these three descriptions we would be very

Table 1.1
Summary of Characteristics of Family 82

Nationality:	Canadian
Husbands Occupation:	Laborer
Wife at:	Home
Home Owned:	No

Age and Sex of Children

Number Aged:	Total	Number of Children	
Males 12, 10, 7, 5, 3, 1	6	At Work	1
Females 14	1	In School	0
Total --	7	At Home	3
		Unknown	3

Income Source	Amount	Percent of Total Family Income
Husband's Income	$350.00	66.7%
Wife's Income	—	—
Children's Income	$175.00	33.3%
Other Sources	—	—
TOTAL	$525.00	100.0%

Expenditures

Item	Amount	Percent of Total Family Income
Food	$437.54	83.3%
Non-Food Items	$196.57	37.4%
Total Expenditures	$634.11	120.7%

Expenditures for:

Rent, Heat, Lighting	$ 79.92	15.2%
Clothing	$ 58.00	11.1%
Furniture	$ 20.00	3.8%
Taxes and Insurance	$ 1.25	0.2%
"Non-Essentials"	$ 14.00	2.7%
Sickness and Death	$ 20.00	3.8%
"Other"	$ 3.60	0.7%

End-of-Year:	Deficit of $109.11
Interviewer Comments	"House poorly furnished"

hesitant to describe any of the three households as typical of the larger group of households.

TO THE READER

The purpose of this section is threefold: to suggest means by which an improved impression of the characteristics and conditions of the families can be gained; to call attention to the need for sensitivity to possible errors and discrepancies that may or may not be present in historical source materials; and to suggest problems confronted in interpreting and making sense of source material.

A better sense of family income and expenditure patterns can be gained through comparison with modern-day spending and income patterns. To do so family expenditures and income must be adjusted to reflect changes in prices. As we know, prices have increased greatly since the late 1880s. A given amount of money will purchase fewer commodities and services today than that amount would purchase in the late 1880s. The purchasing power, or value, of money has declined as prices have inflated. Thus spending and income in the latter 1880s must be converted to "current dollars," or the reverse, if meaningful comparisons are to be made.

These conversions can be made through a few simple operations using the Consumer Price Index (CPI) maintained by the United States Bureau of Labor Statistics. The Consumer Price Index provides an index value for each year from 1800 to the present. The index values afford a means to compare monetary values and prices from one year to another.[2]

To compare price and monetary values for particular years, the index values for the relevant years are employed. The Consumer Price Index values are the same, 27, for each of the years 1888, 1889, 1890 during which the families were interviewed and the data collected. The index value for 1985 is 322.2. These index values indicate that prices in 1985 were, *on average*, 11.9 (322.2 divided by 27) times higher than in the late 1880s. Conversely, prices in the late 1880s were on the average .084 (27 divided by 322.2) those of 1985.

The operations required to convert expenditures and income for any year for which the index is available into current dollars for a later year can readily be seen. The index value for the later year is divided by the index value for the earlier year and the number to be converted multiplied by the result. In this way the yearly income of the family described in the letter quoted above can be converted to 1985 dollars. The index value for 1985 (322.2) is divided by the index value for the earlier years (27) yielding 11.9, and the family's income ($576.00) multiplied by 11.9 with $6,854.40 as the result. In terms of the index, in other words, a yearly income of $576.00 in the late 1880s would be the approximate equivalent of a yearly income of $6,854.40 in 1985.

Income and expenditures for later years can be converted to current dollars for earlier years through essentially the same operations. We know from *The Statistical Abstract of the United States* for 1987 that median household income in 1985 was $23,618. Half of the households in the United States had incomes greater than that amount and half had incomes of less than that amount. Median household income in 1985 can be converted to late 1880s dollars in the following fashion. The index value 27 is divided by the index value for 1985 (322.2) with .084 as the result. $23,618 is multiplied by .084 with $1,983.91 as the result. In other words, the median family income in 1985 was the equivalent in purchasing power of an income of about $1,983.91 in the late 1880s.

These comparisons clearly suggest that the incomes of the families considered in this chapter were very low by contemporary standards. A yearly income of $6,854 (the income of the family described in the letter converted to current 1985 dollars) for a family of seven would be considered low indeed today and would in fact be well below the currently accepted "poverty line." Even the higher income family described in the chapter (Household 121) would have yearly earnings of only $12,411.70 in current 1985 dollars, well below the median for all households in the United States and only somewhat above the "poverty line" for a family of five. The comparisons, then, suggest a rather dismal picture of the three families discussed in the chapter.

The validity of these comparisons can certainly be questioned. Questions can easily be seen, for example, by considering the nature and basis of the Consumer Price Index. In rather complex ways the index value for a given year is calculated on the basis of the prices during that year of a "market basket" of commodities and services, and the amounts of those commodities and services, that are seen as typically purchased by individuals and families. As prices of the components of the market basket fluctuate from year to year, the index goes up or down. The question is the "content" of the market basket, and the standards or expectations which the content is intended to reflect.

Standards of living and expectations have changed and new commodities and services have become available since the late 1880s. In the late 1880s, no one bought or expected to buy a television set, a radio, or an automobile. Fewer people at that time than today expected to take extended vacations and few expected to have periodic medical or dental examinations. Standards of living were lower in the late 1880s than today and expectations as to what constituted an adequate standard of living were also lower.

The point is that the comparisons reflect two components of change. One is change in price levels and the fact that a given amount of money would purchase more goods and services in the late 1880s than the same amount would today. The second component involves differences in living standards and expectations. The content of the Consumer Price Index market basket is different for different time periods reflecting differing standards and expectations. The question is, how good a standard of living would a given income level support in the late 1880s? This is, of course, one of the primary questions addressed in the pages that follow.

The final task in this section is really something of a mystery and might, in fact, be described as "The Case of the Missing Family Member." For many of us the letter reproduced in this chapter is a striking and convincing document. The clarity and directness with which it is written, the precise and extensive detail which it provides, the colorful explanations of real life situations which it gives combine to evoke an impression of accuracy, a feeling of empathy, and a sense that we now have an understanding of what things were really like.

But, as readers will have observed, the letter includes an apparent discrepancy that may undermine our sense of credibility. At three points the letter indicates that the family included seven members. In giving the number of children, however, four are indicated—of ages 2, 4, 6 and 7. Four children plus the wife and husband, the only two adults that are explicitly referred to, sum to six family members not seven. The question is, what happened to the seventh family member?

Three possibilities will readily come to mind and additional thought will suggest others. One possibility is that an error was made in copying the letter for this chapter. As it happens, a check against the original source indicates that the reproduction is accurate. On the other hand, the source actually used is, in a sense, not the original source. The source employed is itself a published copy of the original letter which apparently has not survived. It is possible, then, that an error was made in printing the published version. If that was the case, does it mean that the answer to the question is there never was a seventh family member?

A second possibility is more distressing. Does the discrepancy lead, or lend weight, to the conclusion that the letter is fictitious and was crafted by someone in the office of the Commissioner of Labor to lend a little color and human interest to an otherwise dry-as-dust compilation? But this possibility leads to a further question: if someone went to the trouble of constructing such an elaborate and detailed forgery, is it likely that they would have made the silly and obvious mistake of miscounting the number of family members?

The third possibility is more complicated. Is it possible that the reference to "a bottle of Castoria for the baby" in the next to the last paragraph of the letter accounts for the seventh family member? Many of us would not describe a child of two, the youngest child referred to elsewhere in the letter, as a baby, although in some families the youngest child is referred to as "the baby" however old the child may be. It is also the case that when counting the members of families and other groups in these years, infants under one year of age were often not included. One explanation for the practice may have been the relatively low demands that infants imposed upon family resources. Another and more plausible explanation is the very high infant mortality rates characteristic of the time. Infants under one were sometimes not counted because of the likelihood that they would not survive to their first birthday.

— 2 —
FAMILY INCOME

This chapter is concerned with family income. Questions concerning income and its sources are of considerable interest and importance in their own right. In addition, examination of income levels also constitutes a basis for assessing family standards of living and the conditions and quality of family life. At the same time, when grouping families in relation to differences in income, one can begin to identify factors that produced those differences in income, along with the resulting differences in living standards and conditions.

In this chapter three primary questions are addressed: (1) the levels of family income and variations in income levels from one family to the other; (2) the primary sources of family income and the ways in which the families differed in income sources; (3) the differences in income between groups of families and the relations between these differences and other family characteristics. To pursue these questions we could continue to describe individual families after the fashion of the preceding chapter. To do so would soon prove tiresome and would not be useful for present purposes. Even if we described every family and household in this fashion, we would be unable to dependably identify categories of households marked by similar characteristics which differentiated them from other households. However interesting for some purposes, the household-by-household descriptive approach employed in the preceding chapter would not provide a basis for understandable and defensible generalizations about the families.

For these purposes we require other approaches: simple, compact and easily understandable measures that reduce the data and provide summary statements of the amount and relative importance of the sources of income received. Such measures allow us to make general statements about the families and compare them with other groups of families. They afford, as well, a simple means by which we can compare and contrast particular subgroups of families not only with each other, but also with the larger group of 3,043 families. In this way, similarities and differences can be systematically identified and suggestive information gained about factors and processes that produced these differences.

To achieve these goals, we can make use of the numerous measures that are available to summarize and reduce the data. As we employ some of these devices, it will become obvious that information has been both gained and lost. While we lose the capacity to make statements about specific individual households, and some differences and similarities between the households are concealed, we gain the ability with each approach to identify and summarize particular characteristics of the households. It will also be obvious that each approach provides a different perspective. No single approach is enough to provide all needed information, but the combination of perspectives which various approaches provide allows us to make better "sense" of the data and move toward better understanding of the historical past.

FAMILY INCOME

Sources and levels of income can be examined using no more than addition and division. The data collection gives for each family the income, if any, derived from five different sources: the earnings of husbands and of wives and children working outside the household, income from boarders, and income from other unspecified sources. These income categories were apparently intended to be exhaustive of all income received by the families since the five income sources sum to total family income. The first four categories involve income derived from specified sources—working husbands, wives, children, and boarders—while the fifth category records income derived from all other sources. What these other sources were is not given.

A simple way to summarize reported income and its sources is by summing each category to the total for the category. The results are given in table 2.1. The total income received by each family from all sources is also summed and given in table 2.1. The first cell in the first row of the table gives total income received by husbands, which amounted to $ 1,204,964. In similar fashion the total income received by the families from each source is given in the following cells of the row. Total family income received from all sources is given in the final cell of the row.

The distribution of aggregate income from the several sources (the first row of table 2.1) is useful information. As can be seen, in the aggregate, most of the income of these families came from the earnings of husbands; working children constituted the next most important source of family income, while income from working wives, boarders, and other sources was small in relation to income from husbands and working children.

We can see these differences more precisely by calculating total income from each source as percentages of income from all sources. (In other words, by dividing total income from each source by total family income from all sources and multiplying by 100). The results of these calculations are given in the second row of table 2.1. It appears that income from the earnings of husbands constituted 60.1 percent of total family income (the first cell of the second row of the table). Income from working children constituted 26.3

Table 2.1
Aggregate Annual Income of Families, by Source of Income

	Income from Husbands	Income from Working Children	Income from Working Wives	Income from Boarders	Income from Other and Unspecified Sources	Total (Aggregate) Income of the Households
Total Dollar Income, All Families	$1,204,964	$527,180	$78,360	$149,028	$46,916	$2,006,447
Percentage of Income Obtained From Each Source	60.1%	26.3%	3.9%	7.4%	2.3%	100%
Number of Families With Income From Each Source	2,801	1,341	414	729	468	3,043
Percentage of Families with Income from Each Source	92.0%	44.1%	13.6%	24.0%	15.4%	——
Average (Mean) Family Income From Each Source*	$395.98	$173.24	$25.75	$48.97	$15.42	$659.36

*Calculated by dividing total dollar income from each source, and for the aggregate income of the households, by the total number of families (3,043).

percent (the second cell of the second row), and so on. Clearly, other and unspecified sources, the fifth cell in the row, contributed only a small amount to the aggregate income of this group of families, as was the case with boarders as well.

We can gain additional clarification of income levels and sources by further use of these same operations. As we would expect, not all families had income from all of the five sources. The total number of families with income from each source is given in the third row of table 2.1, and the fourth row gives the same information as percentages. As we can see from the two rows, most families (2,801, or 92% of all families) received income from the earnings of husbands. A substantially smaller number and percentage of the families received income from wives working outside the home, from boarders, and from unspecified sources. The number and percentage of families with income from working children were larger but still markedly smaller than the number and percentage with income from the earnings of husbands.

By dividing total income from each income source by the total number of families, mean (average) family income from each source can be calculated. Mean total family income can also be calculated, by dividing total family income from all sources by the total number of families. These means are given in the final row of table 2.1. As the table indicates, mean family income from the earnings husbands is substantially higher than mean family income from the other sources. Here again, mean income from working children, although lower than the mean income of husbands, is higher than mean income from other sources.

Taken together, the calculations suggest several family characteristics. Taken as a group, the families apparently did not have significant sources of income aside from the wages of family members. In other words, they were primarily dependent for their livelihoods and well being upon the earnings of family members. The incidence of wives employed outside the home and the proportion of family income derived from working wives were both lower than is the case today. The calculations give us no clue as to the reasons for this difference. In themselves, the calculations provide no indication of whether the low incidence of wives working outside the home is a reflection of scarcity of employment opportunities for women, a preference that wives not work outside the home, or of some other factor.

The calculations suggest the central importance of the earnings of husbands to family livelihood, although here some qualifications are necessary. On the basis of the first two rows of the table we might conclude, for example, that husbands were the primary "breadwinners" among these families. It is possible, although unlikely, that in a few families husbands had very high incomes, while in most families the earnings of husbands were very low—lower than the income produced by other sources. This possibility is reduced but not entirely ruled out by the second two rows of the table, which indicate that many more families had income from the earnings of husbands than from other sources. It is still possible, however, that in a few families husbands had very large incomes while in most families husbands' earnings were small in relation to income from other sources. Moreover, we do know on the basis of chapter 1 that in at least one family the earnings of the husband were less than family income from other sources.

The table does show that, in the aggregate, most family income came from the earnings of husbands, and that more families had earnings from the work of husbands than from other sources. It can be said that, in the aggregate, family income from other and unspecified sources was small, that few families had income from these sources, and that average income from these sources was low. It is still possible, on the other hand, that a few families had very large incomes from such sources. While these may seem to be rather nit-picking qualifications, they illustrate the care that must be taken in drawing conclusions based upon calculations such as those that underlie table 2.1.

Further qualifications of a more general nature are also necessary. Summary measures, such as those employed in table 2.1 can convey an unwarranted sense of similarity and uniformity. On the basis of the table it would be possible to conclude that the families were a great deal more similar than they were in fact. As an example, the mean (average) is one of many *measures of central tendency*. These are single numbers that are calculated in particular ways to best summarize the actual values for each case for a particular variable or set of variables. The actual values for each case usually depart widely from the measure of central tendency. Put differently, the mean, or other measure of central tendency, usefully summarizes a variable but at the cost of concealing the variation actually characteristic of the variable.

Examination of table 2.2 illustrates these issues and also provides additional information bearing upon the families. The first column of the table gives the mean income received by the families from each of the five sources of income, the same measure that was employed in the final row of table 2.1. In the case of table 2.2, however, the mean is calculated only for those families that had income from the particular source; families without income from that source are excluded from the calculation. Thus the means in table 2.2 are higher than those in the preceding table.

The next three columns in the table provide information bearing upon the distribution of the several variables and suggest that the families differed rather widely in the amount of income received from the various sources.

The values in the second column of the table indicate the lowest income (minimum value) reported for any family for each of the income categories; the third column gives the highest income (maximum value) reported for any family for each of the categories. The fourth column gives the range of income from the lowest to the highest amounts (maximum value minus minimum value) reported for each category. The final column of the table gives the number of families with income from each source.

Thus the lowest income received by any family was $110 (the second cell in the first row of table 2.2); the highest income received by any family was $2,777 (the third cell of the first row); and the income range $2,667 (the fourth cell of the row). As we can be seen, the range of income for each category is broad, suggesting that the families differed greatly in total income and the amounts of income received from each source.

Table 2.2
Distribution of Annual Family Income by Sources of Income*

	Average (Mean) Income	Minimum Income	Maximum Income	Income Range	Number of Families with Income from This Source
Total Family Income	$659.36	$110.00	$2,777.00	$2,667.00	3,043
Income from Husbands	$430.19	$ 10.00	$1,937.00	$1,927.00	2,801
Income from Working Children	$393.12	$ 10.00	$1,764.00	$1,754.00	1,341
Income from Working Wives	$189.28	$ 5.00	$ 606.00	$ 601.00	414
Income from Boarders	$204.43	$ 7.00	$1,650.00	$1.643.00	729
Income from Other and Unspecified Sources	$100.25	$ 2.00	$1,200.00	$1,198.00	468

*All figures in this table were calculated using only families having income from the respective sources.

On the basis of these tables we can draw several conclusions. It is reasonably certain, as was undoubtedly expected, that husbands were the primary sources of income for this group of families. In the aggregate, income from the earnings of husbands was greater than income from other sources and more families had income from the earnings of husbands than from other sources. The mean earnings of husbands are higher than in the case of the other sources and the maximum income value for husbands is higher than the equivalent values for the other income sources. Obviously, then, most of the families would have suffered severe income loss if the husband who, it was surmised, often worked in hazardous conditions lost their employment, became sick, or were injured or killed.

While husbands were the primary sources of income, we can also see that some families had significant income from other sources. By comparing the minimum and maximum values in table 2.2 we can see that in some families income from working children and, less frequently, from working wives, boarders, and unspecified sources exceeded the earnings of husbands. A few working women did have higher earnings than the mean earnings of male heads of households. The mean earnings of women were, however, well below those of men. The suggestion is that working women received lower wages than men.

There is no indication at this point that the wages of children were lower than the wages of men. Something can be said about the income and wages of working wives since there is no more than one working wife in a family. On the other hand, in some families more than one child worked. Tables 2.1 and 2.2 do not distinguish between families with only one working child and those with more than one child at work. Hence the tables tell us nothing of average or median earnings per working child.

An obvious conclusion is that the families varied considerably in income and income sources. More information is needed about this variation and its distribution. The ranges and minimum and maximum values of income given in the preceding tables are measures of distribution. Many other such measures are also available. One method involves dividing the families into subgroups. In table 2.3 we divide the families into four subgroups of approximately equal size (quartiles) in terms of total family income. The 25 percent of the families with the lowest income are combined into one group, the 25 percent with the next to lowest total income into a second group, the 25 percent with the next to highest income into a third group, and the 25 percent with the highest income into a fourth group. The decision to divide the families into quartiles is arbitrary. We could have used, for example groups of ten percent (deciles), or 20 percent (quintiles).

As the first three rows of the table indicate the total income of the lowest quartile varied from $110 to $457 per year, a range of $347.00; that of the second quartile from $457.20 to $590 per year, a $132.80 range; that of the third from $591 to $799.70 per year, or a $208.70 range; and that of the fourth and highest income quartile from $800 to $2,777 per year, a range of $1,977.00. Obviously, the income range for the fourth quartile is much broader than the income ranges of the other quartiles suggesting both the greater diversity of these families and the probability that a few of them had unusually high incomes in comparison with the rest. Similarly, the income range for the lowest quartile, although narrower than the range of the fourth quartile, is broader than that of either of the two middle income quartiles suggesting greater diversity at the lower end of the income spectrum.

The fourth row of the table gives the mean income for each income quartile. The mean income for the fourth and highest income quartile is approximately twice that of the second quartile and almost three times greater than that of the first quartile. The mean income of the fourth quartile is also relatively low in relation to the income range for that group, suggesting once again that a few families in this group had comparatively high incomes. The fifth row of the table gives the total income received by each group of families, and the sixth gives these totals as percentages of the total income received by all 3,043 families.

These latter percentages can be used as measures of the inequality of income. In these terms, the 25 percent of the 3,043 families with the lowest incomes received only about 14 percent of the total income received by all families. In contrast, the 25 percent of the families with the highest incomes received approximately 40 percent of all family income. On the basis of

Table 2.3
Quartile Distribution of Annual Family Income

	First Quartile ($110-$457)	Second Quartile ($457.20-$590)	Third Quartile ($591-$799.70)	Fourth Quartile ($800-$2,777)
Minimum Income	$110.00	$457.20	$591.00	$800.00
Maximum Income	$457.00	$590.00	$799.70	$2,777.00
Income Range	$347.00	$132.80	$208.70	$1,977.00
Mean Income	$372.37	$522.18	$681.31	$1,059.52
Total Dollar Income	$282,998.00	$396,856.88	$517,117.34	$809,474.51
Total Dollar Income as a Percentage of Aggregate Income of all 3,043 Families	14.1%	19.8%	25.8%	40.3%

table 2.3 we might surmise the families differed rather greatly in standards of living.

The operations used for table 2.3 also provide a means to examine income sources in relation to family income. A logical inference might be that some families enjoyed higher incomes in part because they were able to draw upon more income sources. Table 2.4 provides a partial test of this inference by cross-tabulating family income for the quartile groups in relation to the several income sources. The table gives the percentages of family income derived by each income quartile and by all families from the several income sources given in the data collection. The table should be read across the rows in the following fashion: the 25 percent of the families with the lowest income (the first row of the table) received 76.7 percent of their income from the earnings of husbands, 12.9 percent from working children, 5.2 percent from wives working outside the home, 3.3 percent from boarders, and 1.9 percent from other and unspecified income sources, summing to 100 percent of the income of the group. The other rows of the table can be read in similar fashion.

Comparison of the rows in table 2.4 supports our inference. Families with higher incomes derived larger amounts from sources other than the earnings of husbands and were, in other words, less dependent on husbands for their livelihoods. As we move down the first column of the table, from the lowest to the highest income quartile, the percentage of income from the earnings of husbands declines. In contrast, income from working children and boarders increases as we move from the lower to the higher income quartiles. Income from other and unspecified sources remains relatively constant. Families in each quartile apparently derived approximately

Table 2.4
Sources of Family Income by Quartile Distribution
of Total Family Income

Percentage of Total Family Income from:

	Husbands	Working Children	Working Wives	Boarders	Other and Unspecified Sources	Total
First Quartile	76.7%	12.9%	5.2%	3.3%	1.9%	100%
Second Quartile	74.8%	14.1%	4.5%	5.0%	1.6%	100%
Third Quartile	63.9%	22.5%	5.0%	6.4%	2.2%	100%
Fourth Quartile	44.6%	39.3%	2.5%	10.7%	2.9%	100%
All Families	60.1%	26.3%	3.9%	7.4%	2.3%	100%

the same percentage of their income from such sources. Income from wives working outside the home also remains relatively constant across the first three income quartiles but drops sharply in the fourth and highest income quartile.

In comparing each quartile, the percentages of all families (the fifth row of the table) indicates the ways in which families in each quartile deviated in income sources from the patterns characteristic of the entire set of families. As can be seen, families in the lowest quartile received a greater proportion of their income from the earnings of husbands, less from working children, more from the earnings of wives, less from boarders, and slightly less from other sources than the entire group of families.

Using table 2.4 we can formulate several hypotheses concerning the sources of variation in income between the several groups and as well as differences in other characteristics of the groups. It can be hypothesized, for example, that the lowest income group was disproportionately composed of families in which husbands and wives were young and there were young children at home. Thus children tended to be too young to work and wives were needed at home to care for the children. The higher income quartiles, it can be hypothesized, were disproportionately composed of families with older husbands and wives and with more children who were old enough to work. We might or might not take the lower percentage of income derived from working wives in the highest income quartile as added support for these hypotheses. A seemingly more obvious inference from table 2.4 would be that to have wives working outside the home was not a preferred means to supplement family income.

REGIONAL AND NATIONAL DIFFERENCES

By combining the families into income categories we can also compare specific groups of families. Historical research and various historical sources indicate that in the latter nineteenth century foreign-stock families and individuals tended to fare less well than the native stock. Thus it is logical to hypothesize that among the families of concern the foreign stock tended to have lower incomes than the native stock and that place of birth and national background were among the factors that influenced levels of family income. (The uncertainties involved in classifying families in this way, as discussed in the Introduction, should be kept in mind.)

Table 2.5 uses the same income quartiles as in tables 2.3 and 2.4 to compare foreign- and native-stock families. In table 2.5 the percentages of foreign- and native-stock families with income levels in each income quartile are given. As the fifth column indicates, the table is percentagized across each row and the cell entries in each row sum to 100 percent. By convention the 100 percent at the end of each row indicates that the table should be read across the rows in the following fashion: of the foreign-stock families (the first row) 17.6 percent had incomes in the first (lowest) income quartile, 23.3 percent had incomes in the second quartile, 24.6 percent had incomes in the third quartile, and 34.5 percent had incomes in the fourth (highest) quartile. The income distribution of the native stock, the second row of the table should be read in similar fashion.

Comparison of the rows in the table suggests that native-stock family income tended to be lower than that of the foreign-stock families. Only 17.6 percent of the foreign-stock families ranked in the lowest income quartile as compared with 32 percent of the native-stock families; only 16.1 of the native-stock families ranked in the highest income quartile as compared with 34.5 percent of the foreign stock. Similar but much smaller differences can be seen in the case of the other income quartiles. The mean income of the foreign-stock families is also higher than that of the native stock, $732.74 as compared with $589.70 (the sixth column of the table).

This is, of course, not the difference that was expected on the basis of our hypothesis. It was hypothesized that the income levels of the foreign-stock families would tend to be lower than those of the native stock. Should these differences be accepted without further question, or is it possible that additional factors need to be considered?

We do need to take other factors into consideration. Table 2.5 does not take into account the regions of the nation in which the families resided. All native-stock and all foreign-stock families are grouped together regardless of the state and region of residence. In the United States of the latter nineteenth century, however, the Southern and, to a lesser degree, the Border states were characterized by lower wages than the Northern states. It was also the case that immigrants from other nations tended to settle in the Northern states in part because of differences in wage levels. Perhaps if

Table 2.5
Income of Native- and Foreign-Stock Families by
Quartile Distribution of Total Family Income

Percentage of Families with Total Family Income in:

	First Quartile	Second Quartile	Third Quartile	Fourth Quartile	Total	Mean Income	Number of Families
Foreign-Stock Families	17.6%	23.3%	24.6%	34.5%	100%	$732.74	1482
Native-Stock Families	32.0%	26.6%	25.3%	16.1%	100%	$589.70	1561

the states and regions in which the families lived and worked are taken into account, then the expected differences in income levels will appear.

Table 2.6 again gives the percentage of families with incomes in the quartile ranges used in preceding tables. In this case, however, the families are classified both as native or foreign stock and in terms of the regions of the nation in which they lived. Families that were of native stock and resided in the Northern states are grouped into one category (the first row of the table), those of foreign stock and residing in the North are grouped in a second category (the second row of the table), native- and foreign-stock families residing in the Border states are grouped into two additional categories, and Southern native- and foreign-stock families are grouped into the fifth and sixth categories. These regional and national groupings are then cross-tabulated against the income quartiles. The fifth column of the table again indicates the way in which the table was constructed and that it should be read in the same fashion as table 2.5. The last two columns of the table provide, respectively, the mean income for each group and the total number of families included in each group.

Like the preceding table, table 2.5 fails to provide support for our original hypothesis, although it does provide additional information. In the South the income of foreign-stock families did tend to be substantially higher (a mean income of almost $700) than that of native-stock families (a mean of $502.71). In these states, however, there were only a very small number of foreign-stock families, as the final column of the table indicates, and it is plausible to assume that these families may have been exceptional in some respects. Much the same can also be said of the foreign-stock families in the Border states.

Table 2.6
Income of Native- and Foreign-Stock by Region and
Quartile Distribution of Total Family Income

Percentage of Families with Total Family Income in:

	First Quartile	Second Quartile	Third Quartile	Fourth Quartile	Total	Mean Income	Number of Families
Northern Native-Stock	20.4%	30.2%	29.4%	20.0%	100%	$638.95	749
Northern Foreign-Stock	17.5%	23.2%	24.6%	34.7%	100%	$734.03	1,450
Border State Native-Stock	27.7%	21.8%	26.1%	24.4%	100%	$644.55	238
Border State Foreign-Stock	26.7%	26.7%	13.3%	33.3%	100%	$644.91	15
Southern Native-Stock	48.8%	23.8%	19.7%	7.7%	100%	$502.71	574
Southern Foriegn Stock	17.6%	23.6%	35.3%	23.5%	100%	$699.80	17

We can also see that the income levels of native-stock families in the Southern states were noticeably below those of either Northern native- or foreign-stock families, suggesting the regional differences in wage levels referred to above. The differences in income between the foreign- and native-stock families in the Northern states were smaller than in the case of the Southern families or than was suggested by the simple comparison of native- and foreign-stock families given in table 2.5. Even so, it does appear, contrary to our hypothesis, that the Northern native-stock families tended to have lower total incomes than the Northern foreign-stock families.

But still other factors need to be taken into consideration. Tables 2.5 and 2.6 concern only total family income. We might suspect that income derived from specific sources would follow a different pattern and show the expected differences between the native- and foreign-stock families. One such possibility is that income from the earnings of husbands, the single most important income source, tended to be lower among the foreign stock than among the native stock. At first glance, comparison of mean income from the earnings of husbands suggests that this was probably not the case. For all foreign-stock families taken as a group the mean income from husbands' earnings was $398.84. For all native-stock families taken as a group mean income from husbands' earnings was $389.45, lower than the equivalent value for all foreign-stock families. These differences, however, may result from the regional wage differences referred to above and reflected in table 2.6.

To explore this possibility, table 2.7 cross-tabulates the regional and national groupings employed in table 2.6 against the quartile distribution of income from the earnings of husbands. For table 2.7, income quartiles are recomputed for the earnings of husbands and the income ranges for each quartile are given in the column headings. Families with no recorded income from husbands' earnings are excluded. (242 families are recorded as without earnings from husbands.)

In preparing table 2.7, the small number of foreign-stock families residing in the Border and Southern states are excluded. The number of such families is very small and they tend to differ from the native stock in these regions. We might therefore think of them as unusual and unrepresentative. Certainly, we would have little confidence in generalizations based upon such small numbers.

Table 2.7 is more nearly in accord with our hypothesis than the preceding tables. In the Northern states the income of native-stock husbands tended to be higher than that of foreign-stock husbands. Only 6 percent of the Northern native-stock families fell into the lowest quartile in terms of husbands' earnings as compared with 20.6 percent of the foreign stock. In contrast, 42.5 percent of the Northern native stock ranked in the highest

Table 2.7

Husbands' Income For Native- And Foreign-stock Families
By Region And By Quartile Distribution Of Husbands' Income

Percentage Of Families With Husbands' Income In:

	First Quartile	Second Quartile	Third Quartile	Fourth Quartile	Total	Mean Husbands' Income	Number Of Families
	($0-$290)	($290.01-$396.90)	($396.01-$510)	($510.01-$1,937)			
Northern Native-Stock Families	6.0%	17.1%	34.4%	42.5%	100%	$498.12	749
Northern Foreign-Stock Families	20.6%	29.2%	27.7%	22.5%	100%	$401.50	1,450
Border State Native-Stock Families	31.5%	30.7%	16.4%	21.4%	100%	$375.34	238
Southern Native-Stock Families	59.6%	21.4%	11.3%	7.7%	100%	$253.49	574

quartile of husbands' earnings while only 22.5 percent of the foreign stock were in this category. Put differently, when region of residence is taken into account, as in table 2.7, it does appear that in the North the earnings of native-stock husbands were higher than those of the foreign stock. The earnings of native-stock husbands in the Border and Southern states appear below those of either the foreign or native stock in the North.

GENERALIZATIONS AND QUALIFICATIONS

On first consideration we may find the analytic results presented in this chapter odd and even contradictory. They provide a basis, however, for several tentative conclusions and may also suggest further inferences. Among these families, the data suggest, the total family income of foreign-stock families tended to be higher than the total income of native-stock families. These differences in income persist even when regional differences in wages are taken into account. The consistent pattern in all regions is higher total income among foreign-stock families, not the pattern that was expected.

In contrast, the earnings of native-stock husbands in the North tended to be higher than the earnings of foreign-stock husbands in that region. We also know that families with higher total income tended to have income from a greater number of sources in addition to the earnings of husbands. Such families drew larger percentages of their incomes from these alternative sources and particularly from working children. On the basis of this information, can we draw inferences concerning differences in families or family practices between foreign- and native-stock families? Can we infer, for example, that Northern foreign-stock families tended to be larger with more older children and older wives and husbands than native-stock families? Alternatively, can we infer that family practices differed, and that the Northern foreign stock tended to send children to work more frequently and at an earlier age than the native stock?

TO THE READER

One purpose of this chapter is to examine differences in sources and levels of income between different regional and nationality groups. For this purpose, the families were first grouped into two nationality categories, foreign and native stock (table 2.5). The families were then further divided (table 2.6) into six smaller categories taking into account their area of residence as well as their nationality. The categories employed were (1) native-stock families residing in the Northern states; (2) foreign-stock families residing in the Northern states; (3) native-stock families residing in the Border states; (4) foreign-stock families in the Border states; (5) native-stock Southern families; and (6) foreign-stock Southern families. Since the Border states and the South proved to include only a small number of foreign-stock families, these categories were subsequently omitted from the examination.

The remaining categories—Northern native and foreign stock, Border state and Southern native stock—present additional difficulties. One is that the Northern foreign-stock group is both large (1,450 families) and heterogeneous. All told, nineteen different nationality groups are included in this category, although some are represented by at most a small number of families (see table 1 of the Introduction). It is highly likely that these groups differed from each other in various of their characteristics. One of our goals in this section is to begin identifying the ways in which more specific groups of families differed from each other.

For this purpose, the families are recategorized. The Northern native-stock, Border state native-stock, and Southern native-stock categories are retained. The Northern foreign-stock families are subdivided into five categories. The French Canadian families are grouped in one category. The families labeled only "Canadian" are grouped in a separate category. The meaning of these labels is unclear, although it might be assumed that the first group was composed of French speaking Canadians and the second of English speaking Canadians. The data, however, do not so indicate. The Irish are retained as a separate category, and the English, Scots, and Welsh are grouped into a single category and, with apologies to the Scots and Welsh, described as British. All continental European nationalities are grouped into a fifth category and labeled continental Europeans.

It should be clear that some of these categories, and particularly the continental European category, are also heterogeneous. The small number of families of some nationalities makes it necessary to combine groups that are disparate in at least some of their characteristics. The categories and the number of families in each are as follows: Northern Native Stock, 749; French Canadians, 226; Canadian, 96; British, 443; Irish, 464; Continental European, 221; Border State Native Stock, 238; and Southern Native Stock, 574. (Families in a ninth category, the 32 foreign-stock families residing in the Southern and Border States, are not included because of the small numbers involved.)

Our goal is to better determine how these groups differed in terms of levels and sources of income. As a prior step, however, reading in other sources should be used to arrive at expectations (or hypotheses) concerning the differences that are likely to be found. That is, which group would we expect to have the lowest or highest income, which group would we expect to draw the most or least income from sources other than the earnings of husbands? In formulating expectations thought should be given to such issues as language and cultural differences and the likelihood of discriminatory treatment by other groups.

As a first step, table 2.8A gives the aggregate total income received by the families in each of the eight regional and nationality categories along with the aggregate income received from each of the five income sources. Also given is the number of families in each category that reported income from each of the several sources and the total number of families in each regional and nationality category.

Table 2.8A provides much useful and interesting information about the families but also has a number of limitations. The table does not, for example, allow reliable assessment of the relative importance of the several income sources for the various regional and national groups. The problem is that the number of families differs from one group to the other. The Northern native-stock families received a greater amount of income from the earnings of husbands than did any of the other regional and nationality groups. Similarly, more Northern native-stock families had income from husbands than any other category.

This is, of course, as we would expect. The Northern native-stock category includes a larger number of families than any other group. It is not surprising, therefore, that the total earnings of native-stock husbands were greater than those of husbands in the other groups. The question is whether the earnings of Northern native-stock husbands were relatively greater than the earnings of other categories of husbands taking into account differences in the number of husbands in each category? Put differently, the question is how did the several regional and nationality groups differ in terms of their relative dependence on the various income sources, taking into account the number of families in each category and the total income received by each category?

We can address questions of the relative importance of the several income sources in straightforward fashion. Obviously, the percentage of total income received by each category from each income source can be calculated by dividing the aggregate income received from each source by the total income received by the category of family and multiplying by 100. The percentage of families in each group with income from each source can be calculated in similar fashion. These operations have been carried out for four groups of families and the results recorded in table 2.8B. For purposes of comparison, the same operations should be carried out for additional groups of families and also recorded in table 2.8B. Before doing so, predictions should be made concerning how these additional groups will compare with the groups already recorded in table 2.8B and with each other.

A second step in examining the eight regional and nationality groups is to compare the relative levels of earnings of husbands. For this purpose, table 2.9A gives the numbers of families in each group in terms of the quartile distribution of the earnings of husbands (the quartile distribution is

Table 2.8A
Aggregate Annual Income of Families, by Source of Income, Nationality and Region of Residence

	Income from Husbands	Income from Working Children	Income from Working Wives	Income from Boarders	Income from Other and Unspecified Sources	Total (Aggregate) Income of Households
Total Dollar Income:						
Northern Native-Stock	$373,091	$51,400	$21,568	$21,150	$11,363	$478,572
Northern French Canadian	$83,852	$61,685	$6,515	$14,542	$2,812	$169,407
Northern Canadian	$32,390	$22,942	$3,149	$4,567	$3,120	$66,168
Northern British	$209,057	$74,077	$14,207	$23,491	$6,976	$327,807
Northern Irish	$167,034	$131,699	$9,918	$36,868	$8,826	$354,345
Northern Continental European	$89,847	$38,674	$5,063	$8,385	$4,654	$146,623
Border State Native-Stock	$89,331	$43,867	$2,760	$15,290	$2,153	$153,402
Southern Native-Stock	$145,506	$99,399	$14,974	$22,935	$6,738	$288,553
Number of Families with Income From Each Source:						
Northern Native-Stock	729	145	92	103	111	749
Northern French Canadian	226	111	36	60	32	226
Northern Canadian	85	49	15	25	20	96
Northern British	428	191	70	90	56	443
Northern Irish	411	272	61	149	79	464
Northern Continental European	209	88	25	42	41	221
Border State Native-Stock	222	134	15	84	27	237
Southern Native-Stock	460	338	98	166	100	574

Table 2.8b
Percentage of Income of Families, by Source of Income, Nationality and Region of Residence

	Income from Husbands	Income from Working Children	Income from Working Wives	Income from Boarders	Income from Other and Unspecified Sources	Total
Percentage of Income From Each Source:						
Northern Native-Stock	78.0%	10.7%	4.5%	4.4%	2.4%	100%
Northern French Canadian	49.5%	36.4%	3.8%	8.6%	1.7%	100%
Northern Canadian	48.9%	34.7%	4.8%	6.9%	4.7%	100%
Northern British	63.8%	22.6%	4.3%	7.2%	2.1%	100%
Northern Irish						
Northern Continental European						
Border State Native-Stock						
Southern Native-Stock						
Percentage of Families With Income From Each Source:						
Northern Native-Stock	97.3%	19.4%	12.2%	13.8%	14.8%	--
Northern French Canadian	100.0%	49.1%	15.9%	26.5%	14.2%	--
Northern Canadian	88.5%	51.0%	15.6%	26.0%	20.8%	--
Northern British	96.6%	43.1%	15.8%	20.3%	12.6%	--
Northern Irish						
Northern Continental European						
Border State Native-Stock						
Southern Native-Stock						

the same as in table 2.7). As we can see, 45 of the Northern native-stock families ranked in the first quartile of husbands' income, 128 in the second quartile, 258 in the third, and so on.

Our question is again the relative differences between the families while holding the number of families in each regional and nationality group constant. The final column of table 2.9A gives the total number of families in each regional and nationality group to allow calculation of the percentages of families in each quartile. The calculations have again been carried out for four of the eight groups and are given in table 2.9B. The same calculations should be carried out for additional groups. Before doing so, hypotheses should be formulated concerning the ways in which these groups will compare with each other and with the groups for which calculations have already been carried out and recorded in the table. The reasons underlying these hypotheses should also be formulated.

It will be obvious that information provided by tables 2.8A through 2.9B can be employed to address a number of questions concerning differences in income levels and sources between the eight regional and nationality groups. It is equally obvious that on the basis of this information some questions can be addressed with greater assurance than others, and some interesting questions cannot be addressed at all. The following are some of the questions that might be addressed.

1. Which of the eight groups was relatively best off in terms of total family income?
2. Which of the eight groups was most dependent upon the income of husbands, on the income of children employed outside the home, on the income of wives working outside the home?
3. Is it likely that some groups of families tended to have larger numbers of children than other groups? If so, which group is likely to have had the largest number of children, the next largest number, and so on?
4. Is it likely that some groups tended to place a higher value on the education of children while other groups tended to a lower value on education but a higher value on additional income? If so, what group of families tended to value income most and which tended to value education most?
5. Is there any indication that some groups more strongly preferred that wives not work outside the home than other groups? If so, which group?

In attempting to answer these questions, thought should be given to the specific arguments and data that support the answers. Similarly, possible qualifications to the answers should be considered. It will be recognized that some questions can be answered with greater confidence than others and it is possible that some of the questions cannot be answered at all on the basis of the available information. Thought should be given, of course, to the reasons for differing degrees of confidence in particular answers to particular questions. What other questions can be addressed using the information given in tables 2.8A through 2.9B and, for that matter, in the tables presented earlier in this chapter?

Table 2.9
Number and Percentage of Families with Husbands' Earnings in
Each Quartile by Nationality and Region of Residence

Table 2.9A: Number of Families

	First Quartile	Second Quartile	Third Quartile	Fourth Quartile	Number of Families	Mean Income of Husbands
Northern Native-Stock	45	128	258	318	749	$498.12
Northern French Canadian	44	91	63	28	226	$371.03
Northern Canadian	31	26	25	14	96	$337.40
Northern British	57	82	151	153	443	$471.91
Northern Irish	124	150	111	79	464	$359.99
Northern Continental European	43	75	52	51	221	$406.55
Border State Native Stock	75	73	39	51	238	$375.34
Southern Native Stock	342	123	65	44	574	$253.49

Table 2.9B: Percentage of Families

	First Quartile	Second Quartile	Third Quartile	Fourth Quartile	Total
Northern Native Stock	6.0%	17.1%	34.4%	45.5%	100%
Northern French Canadian	19.5%	40.3%	27.8%	12.4%	100%
Northern Canadian	32.3%	27.1%	26.0%	14.6%	100%
Northern British	12.9%	18.5%	34.1%	34.5%	100%
Northern Irish					
Northern Continental European					
Border State Native Stock					
Southern Native Stock					

— 3 —

FAMILY SPENDING

By almost any modern standard the income of these families seems low. Their income levels appear low in terms of our personal experience and much below the levels of income that are familiar in our own time. It is not meaningful, however, to discuss income levels without considering how income was actually spent and what given levels of income would buy. One of our goals, moreover, is to assess standards of living among industrial workers in the late nineteenth century. Income is a useful *indicator* of standards of living, but income is not *synonymous* with standard of living. A variety of factors influence—or mediate—the relationship between income and standard of living. Because of mediating factors, some families and individuals are able to enjoy a better standard of living than others even though income is the same. (It would be useful to give thought to what some of these mediating factors might be.)

The Consumer Price Index is useful for these purposes. We can use the index to translate income levels for the years from 1888 through 1890 into current dollars (and the reverse). Since we have intuitive notions of the standards of living that a given income will support in the present day, we can gain some sense of the standards of living that could be supported by given levels of income at the end of the 1880s. The adequacy of the Index, however, is often questioned as a means to compare the purchasing power of income even over short periods in the contemporary era. Its adequacy as a means to compare and translate income across one hundred years is even more questionable, as the discussion at the close of chapter 1 suggests.

We must therefore examine directly the reported expenditures of the families. The broad questions concern the amounts and proportions of income spent for various purposes and differences in expenditure patterns in relation to income levels and to the national origins and regions of residence of the families. These questions in turn are preliminary steps in assessing the standards of living of the families, for identifying factors that affected living standards and for comparing the relative well-being and prosperity of specific groups.

EXPENDITURE PATTERNS

The data collection gives the amounts spent by the families for a variety of commodities and purposes. One way to assess the economic situation of the families is in terms of expenditures for necessary and non-necessary (discretionary) purposes. We would probably think of expenditures for food, clothing, housing, and death and medical care as necessary. We would expect that families that were better off economically would spend smaller proportions of their income for necessities and larger proportions for non-necessities. Spending by families that were less well off economically would tend to follow the opposite pattern. Thus the amounts spent for necessities as opposed to non-necessities provide a clue to the economic situation of the families.

This approach is employed in table 3.1 which groups expenditures into six categories. All expenditures for food are grouped into a single category; household expenditures (including rent, heat, lighting, taxes, and furniture and utensils) are combined in a second category; clothing expenditures are combined into a third category; and expenditures for sickness and death are retained as a fourth category. A fifth category is composed of discretionary expenditures and includes expenditures for life and property insurance, labor and other organizations, religious expenses, charity, books and newspapers, amusements and vacation, intoxicating liquors, and tobacco. "Other costs" is retained as a sixth category since it includes unspecified and undifferentiated expenditures. These six spending categories are exhaustive.

Difficulties in classifying expenditures as discretionary or necessary, as suggested in chapter 1, must be kept in mind. Some of the expenditures grouped in the discretionary category will undoubtedly seem more discretionary than others. It is certain as well that some expenditures for food and clothing, as examples, were actually discretionary. Families undoubtedly sometimes bought more expensive cuts of meat or more expensive clothing than was actually necessary. Classifications of this sort cannot be completely accurate and thought should be given to the analytic consequences of likely departures from accuracy.

Table 3.1
Aggregate Annual Expenditures of Families, by Type of Expense

Expenditures for:

	Food	Household Costs	Clothing	Sickness and Death	Discretionary Purposes	Other Costs	Total Family Expenditures
Percentage of Total Family Income Spent On Each Category of Expenditure	42.4%	19.7%	14.7%	3.0%	6.3%	5.8%	92.0%*
Cumulative Percentage of Total Family Income Spent on Categories of Expenditures	42.4%	62.1%	76.8%	79.8%	86.1%	91.9%	91.9%
Mean Dollar Expenditure	$279.82	$129.65	$97.15	$21.50	$41.44	$38.71	$605.60
Number of Families with Expenditures in Each Category	3,043	3,043	3,042	2,758	3,038	3,008	3,403

*Total expenditures do not equal 100 percent of total family income because the 3,043 families as a group had surplus income over their reported expenditures (see the discussion and Tables that follow).

Table 3.1 gives (in the first row) the percentage of the total income of the 3,043 families that was reported as spent for commodities, services, and activities in each category. Subsequent rows give the cumulative percentage of income spent across the set of categories, average and median expenditures in each category, and the number and percentages of families with expenditures in each category. As we see, purchase of food was the largest family expenditure; over 40 percent of total family income went for that purpose. Expenditures for household costs were next largest, followed by spending for clothing. Costs associated with death and sickness, discretionary purposes, and other and unspecified purposes were small. All families had expenditures for food, and nearly all had expenditures for clothing, household costs, and discretionary purposes. Not all families had expenditures for death and sickness and other and unspecified purposes, although most did.

Approximately 80 percent of family income was spent for necessities (the cumulative percentage row in the table). Only about six percent remained for what we have treated as discretionary purposes and another six percent was expended in the other and unspecified category. Even if we assume that some expenditures in the food, household, clothing, and other costs categories were not necessary, we can still see that little family income was spent for discretionary purposes.

The data also indicate that for most families, annual income and expenditures did not balance, as we would expect. The magnitude and incidence of end-of-year surpluses in relation to deficits is an obvious clue to the economic conditions of the families. For purposes of interpretation, we might take end-of-year surpluses as family savings during the year, the amounts that the families were able to lay aside for the future, or, perhaps, to repay past debts. In this interpretation, the families were able to save in total something over $220,000, or approximately 11 percent of the total income of all families. Family deficits (or debts) amounted to about $57,000, or approximately three percent of total family income. Gross debts subtracted from gross savings left net savings of approximately $163,000, or about eight percent of family income. As a group the families ended the year "in the black" with total savings in excess of total debts. In the aggregate, total debts were small in relation to total savings. About 57 percent of the families ended the year in a surplus position, approximately nine percent "broke even," and fully a third (34 percent) had an end-of-year deficit.

We should ponder the meaning of the budget deficits reflected in the data. Many families today end the year in debt rather than with increased savings. Frequently, these are debts accrued through buying a home, an automobile, major durable commodities, or through the costs of educating children, rather than through poverty, mismanagement, or "living beyond their means." In other words, at least some family debts today can be seen as "provident" and, indeed, as a form of saving since they involve accumulation of valuable possessions or meeting longer-term needs. It is possible that the end-of-year deficits of some of these families were similar in nature and involved accumulation of possessions. The likelihood that this was the case needs to be considered in light of the lower incidence of options for credit and installment buying in the latter nineteenth century than today.

Unfortunately, the data collection gives us no direct indication of why the families accrued deficits or what the excess of expenditures went to buy. We can, however, gain suggestive information by considering expenditure patterns among the families in relation to income. Expectations in this case need to be carefully considered. We would probably expect that lower-income families would spend a higher proportion of income on necessities than would higher-income families. If this proved to be the case, and if deficits were larger and occurred more frequently among lower-income families, would it be plausible to assume that deficits were accrued for the kind of provident purposes referred to above? Would it be more sensible to assume that deficits occurred because income was too small to meet necessary costs of living? In contrast, if deficits occurred among families with relatively low expenditures for food and other necessities but high expenditures for discretionary purposes, would it be more likely that the deficits were for provident purposes or were due instead to mismanagement or excessively "high" living?

To explore these issues the same income quartiles are employed in table 3.2 as in table 2.3. Table 3.2 gives the total amounts spent in each of the expenditure categories by the four different income groups. Additional rows in the table give total end-of-year surpluses and deficits, and the final rows present the numbers of families that ended the year with surpluses, deficits, or "broke even." Table 3.3 displays the same information as percentages.

As income increased, table 3.2 suggests, expenditures in all categories also increased. The highest income category spent a greater amount for food than the third and next highest income quartile which had higher expenditures for food than the second income quartile. The first and lowest income quartile had the lowest spending for food. The other expenditure categories follow a similar pattern; in general, the higher the income level the greater the amount that was spent in each category. As we would predict, the aggregate end-of-year deficits decrease across the quartile income categories; the lowest income group had the largest deficits; the highest income group had the smallest deficits. The size of the net end-of-year surplus was also related to income level. The highest income quartile had the largest net surplus and included the largest number of families with surpluses. The net surplus and the number of families with surpluses decline from the highest to the lowest income category.

These results are hardly surprising. Total expenditures in all categories were positively related to income; as income increased, the families tended to spend more in each expenditure category. The picture is different when expenditures are treated as percentages of income (table 3.3). Viewed in this way, some expenditures are inversely related to income. The percentage of income spent on food, housing, and sickness and death tends to decrease moving from the lowest to the highest income quartiles. The lowest income quartile, for example, spent 49 percent of total income on food as compared to 39 percent in the highest income quartile. Summing down the column, the lowest income quartile spent approximately 95 percent of all income on necessities (food, household costs, clothing, sickness and death); the highest quartile spent only about 72 percent of total income for these purposes, and the intermediate income categories fell in between.

Table 3.2
Aggregate Annual Expenditures of Families, by Category
of Expenditure and by Quartile Distribution of Family Income

Families with Total Annual Income in:

	First Quartile	Second Quartile	Third Quartile	Fourth Quartile
Food	$138,826.31	$179,470.34	$217,261.56	$315,919.09
Household Costs	74,223.34	92,697.71	104,356.75	123,253.08
Clothing	40,307.74	55,931.39	76,415.09	122,873.60
Sickness and Death	11,737.56	13,281.75	15,872.73	18,407.65
Discretionary Purposes	16,969.45	24,144.10	32,703.07	52,080.29
Other Costs	15,269.43	20,535.87	30,136.79	50,506.77
Total Family Expenditures	$297,333.75	$386,007.67	$476,589.92	$682,905.42
End-of-Year Surpluses	$ 8,240.00	$ 25,344.00	$ 52,853.00	$134,932.00
End-of-Year Deficits	22,577.00	14,539.00	12,448.00	8,378.00
Number of Families with End-of-Year Surpluses	256	399	492	605
Number of Families with End-of-Year Deficits	441	276	204	118
Number of Families which "Broke Even" at End of the Year	63	85	63	41

Discretionary spending is more surprising. In table 3.2, aggregate discretionary expenditures appeared progressively higher with each level of income. As table 3.3 indicates, the families also tended to spend slightly higher percentages of income for discretionary purposes moving from the lowest to the highest income category, but the differences are minuscule. Across the four income quartiles, from the lowest to the highest, discretionary spending ranged between 6.0 and 6.4 percent—hardly meaningful differences given the likely error present in the data.

As the seventh row of the table indicates, higher-income families tended to spend a smaller percentage of income than lower-income families. Families in the lowest quartile spent approximately 105 percent of income (a net deficit); families in the highest quartile only 84 percent. Thus surpluses, or "savings," increase across the income quartiles from approximately three percent in the lowest quartile to almost 16 percent in the highest. The percentage of families with end-of-year surpluses also increases with income, from approximately 34 percent in the lowest quartile to over 79

Table 3.3
Annual Expenditures of Families Expressed as Percentages
of Total Family Income, by Category of Expenditure
and by Quartile Distribution of Family Income

Families with Total Family Income in:

	First Quartile	Second Quartile	Third Quartile	Fourth Quartile
Food	49.6%	45.3%	42.1%	39.5%
Household Costs	26.6%	23.4%	20.2%	15.2%
Clothing	14.3%	14.1%	14.8%	15.3%
Sickness and Death	4.3%	3.4%	3.1%	2.4%
Discretionary Purposes	6.0%	6.1%	6.3%	6.4%
Other Costs	5.5%	5.2%	5.8%	6.1%
Total Family Expenditures	105.1%	97.3%	92.2%	84.4%
End-of-Year Surpluses	2.7%	6.3%	10.1%	15.9%
End-of-Year Deficits	8.9%	3.7%	2.5%	1.1%
Percentage of Families with End-of-Year Surpluses	33.7%	52.5%	64.8%	79.2%
Percentage of Families with End-of-Year Deficits	58.0%	36.3%	26.9%	15.6%
Percentage of Families which "Broke Even" at End of the Year	8.3%	11.2%	8.3%	5.4%

percent in the highest. The data suggest, in short, that families tended to save rather than spend for discretionary purposes.

The results presented in tables 3.2 and 3.3 are obviously inconclusive, but they are compatible with several tentative generalizations. We might conclude that at the lower income levels, income was barely large enough, and sometimes not large enough, to pay for necessities. Even among families in the highest income quartile, most income was spent for necessities. Discretionary spending apparently did occur even among the lowest income families. But despite the inadequacies of the definitions of necessary and discretionary spending, there is little evidence that excessive discretionary spending was responsible for the end-of-year deficits reported by approximately one-third of the families.

The impression we gain from the data is one of "life at the margin" and of providence rather than profligacy. Economic insecurity was probably a continuing fact of life, as the letter in chapter 1 might also suggest. Even among higher income families, moreover, it appears that income left over after providing for necessities was disproportionately saved rather than spent for discretionary purposes.

These expenditure patterns are in accord with a set of formulations usually referred to as "Engel's Laws" (named after Ernst Engel, a nineteenth century German statistician and not Karl Marx's friend and collaborator, Friedrich Engels). According to these formulations, which are based upon study of numerous family budgets, the amount of income spent by families and individuals for food and other necessities tends to increase as income increases, but the proportion of income spent for food and necessities tends to decline. The poor are compelled to spend most of their income on food and other necessities. As income increases, more and better food tends to be purchased and the amounts spent for food tend to increase, but these amounts constitute diminishing proportions of income. Conversely, as income increases the amounts and proportions of income saved or spent for luxuries tends to increase.

EXPENDITURES AND NATIONALITY

Further questions concern the relationship between the nationality of the families, on the one hand, and their expenditures and economic status, on the other. Recall the suggestion in chapter 2 that characteristics of the areas in which families resided affected their income levels. Thus in examining the relationship between nationality and the expenditures and economic conditions of the families, we must take the region in which the families resided into account.

At this point, our expectations concerning the relationship between the nationality of the families and their economic situation may be somewhat contradictory. On the one hand, a substantial body of historical research and the reports of numerous contemporary observers all suggest that in these years the economic conditions of the native stock tended to be better than the conditions of the foreign stock. On the other hand, our examination of family income in chapter 2 suggests a picture that is in some respects at odds with this view. Contrary to expectations, it appeared in chapter 2 that foreign-stock families had higher total incomes than native-stock families. Native-stock families in the South appeared least well off, but Northern foreign-stock families appeared relatively better off than native-stock families in both the North and the Border states.

As we know, income is not the same thing as economic condition or standard of living. The preceding section suggests, however, two useful indicators of the economic conditions of families. The first of these is their end-of-year financial positions—the degree to which they were able to end the year with surpluses of income as opposed to deficits. The second indicator is the proportion of income spent on food.

The first indicator is employed in table 3.4. The families are divided into quartile groupings in terms of end-of-year surpluses and deficits. (The range of surpluses and deficits for each quartile is given in the column headings of the table.) The families are again grouped in four regional and nationality categories—native-stock families residing in the Northern states, foreign-stock families in the North, native-stock families in the Border States, and Southern native-stock families—and cross-tabulated against the quartile distributions of surpluses and deficits. If our expectations based upon levels of total family income are confirmed, more of the Northern foreign-stock

Table 3.4
Quartile Distribution of End-of-Year Surpluses and Deficits
of Families by Place of Residence and Nativity*

Percentage of Families with End-of-Year Balance in:

	First Quartile (-$551.50 to -$17.45)	Second Quartile (-$17.46 to +$14.30)	Third Quartile ($14.37 to $100.11)	Fourth Quartile ($100.20 to $1,439.23)	Total Number of Families
Northern Native Stock	19.6%	21.6%	28.2%	30.6%	749
Northern Foreign Stock	25.9%	24.1%	22.4%	27.6%	1,450
Border State Native Stock	23.9%	24.8%	29.8%	21.4%	238
Southern Native Stock	30.0%	32.3%	25.3%	12.5%	574

*This table does not include the 32 foreign-stock families residing in the Border and Southern States.

than of the native-stock groups in the North, the South and the Border States ought to rank in the higher quartiles in terms of their end-of-year financial position.

The table does not confirm our expectations. Almost 31 percent of the Northern native-stock families rank in the highest surplus and deficit quartile, more than in the case of any other regional and nationality group. Slightly less than 20 percent of the Northern native-stock families rank in the lowest quartile, fewer than any of the other groups. The poor economic conditions, at least in terms of this indicator, of the Southern native-stock families stand out sharply. The Northern foreign stock appear better off than the Southerners, relatively worse off than the Northern native stock, and similar to the Border state native-stock families.

The proportion of income spent on food also fails to conform to expectations based upon the distribution of total family income. In turning to these matters it will be recalled that use of this indicator rests upon a series of assumptions and empirical investigations of family budgets in various historical contexts. These investigations show that the proportion of family income spent on necessities is inversely related to income level. Examination of the proportion of income which these families spent for necessities constitutes, therefore, a useful means to assess and compare their economic condition and status and a preliminary step in assessing and examining their relative standards of living. Since the relation between income level and proportion of income spent on food is most clear, that proportion can be taken as the most useful indicator for present purposes.

Table 3.5 cross-tabulates the families, by nationality and region of residence, against the quartile distribution of percentage of total income spent on food. The quartiles group the families from low to high in terms of percentage of income spent on food. (The quartile ranges are given in the column heads of the table.) If our expectations derived from the distribution of total family income observed in chapter 2 are confirmed, then relatively more of the Northern foreign-stock families than of families in other groups ought to rank in the first quartile and fewer in the fourth quartile.

Once again the expected distribution does not appear. Thirty-six percent of the Northern native-stock families, as compared to approximately 22 percent of the Northern foreign stock, rank in the lowest quartile in terms of percentage of income spent on food. In contrast, some 30 percent of the Northern foreign-stock families rank in the fourth and highest quartile in percentage of income spent on food as compared to only 18 percent of the Northern native stock. In terms of this indicator, then, the economic conditions of the Northern native-stock families appear relatively better than those of the Northern foreign stock, a finding that is in accord with table 3.4.

Differences between the Border state and Southern native-stock families and the Northern native stock are ambiguous. The impression conveyed by the table is best described as one of similarity among these groups. Surprisingly, compared with other groups the Southern native-stock families appear relatively better off in terms of percentage of income spent on food than they appear either in terms of end-of-year surpluses and deficits or total family income.

CONCLUSIONS AND INFERENCES

The expenditure patterns among the families give an impression of marginality, economic insecurity, and providence. As we saw in chapter 2, the families varied widely in income. Undoubtedly they also varied widely in expenditures and standards of living, and clearly some families were able to live substantially better than others. Even so, most families spent most of their income for necessities. We find little indication that the families spent large amounts for discretionary purposes; the indication is rather that they chose to save to the degree that money was left after paying for necessities. Many of the families did have end-of-year income surpluses, but a third did not and incurred deficits instead. Surpluses, moreover, tended to be small.

Table 3.5
Quartile Distribution of Percent of Income Spent on Food
by Place of Residence and Nativity*

Percentage of Families Whose Food Expenditure
(Calculated as Percent of Total Income) Is In:

	First Quartile (8.59% - 36.29%)	Second Quartile (36.32% - 43.54%)	Third Quartile (43.56% - 50.77%)	Fourth Quartile (50.79% - 149.36%)	Number of Families
Northern Native Stock	35.9%	27.2%	18.8%	18.0%	749
Northern Foreign Stock	21.8%	22.6%	25.9%	29.8%	1,450
Border State Native Stock	18.5%	22.3%	31.1%	28.2%	238
Southern Native Stock	21.1%	29.8%	27.7%	21.4%	574

*This table does not include the 32 foreign-stock families residing in the
Border and Southern States.

It appears that many of the families were seriously vulnerable in the event of loss of income through unemployment or through sickness or injury of family wage earners.

The comparison of the several regional and nationality groups is less clear, and the results of examination of expenditure patterns in this chapter are not entirely in accord with the examination of income levels in chapter 2. On the basis of the levels of family income seen in chapter 2, we might have expected that Northern foreign-stock families would appear relatively better off than other families in terms of surplus and deficit income and in terms of expenditures for food. In fact, this expectation was not fully confirmed. Rather, the Northern native-stock families appear relatively better off than the Northern foreign stock, and the latter families appear at least comparable in economic conditions to the Border state and Southern native stock. The differences, however, are not entirely clear or consistent. We should ponder, therefore, whether this chapter, taken in combination with chapter 2, suggests further inferences concerning differences in family structure and practices between the several regional and nationality groups.

TO THE READER

In this chapter we have taken expenditure patterns as indications of family standards of living and well being, and we have used these patterns to compare the relative well being of particular groups. We have assumed that the smaller the percentage of total income that families spent on food, the better off the families tended to be. Similarly, we have assumed that the end-of-year financial situations of families provide an indication of relative well being. Families with larger surpluses of income in relation to expenditures are taken as better off than families with smaller surpluses or with deficits. Some thought should be given to these assumptions, and to whether and in what ways the comparisons could be misleading.

In this section we continue examining and comparing the living conditions of specific groups using expenditure patterns as indications of relative family well being. The first comparison is between the families of textile workers and groups in our own time. The goal of the comparison is to gain an improved intuitive sense of family living conditions at the end of the 1880s.

Tables 3.1 and 3.3 above give the percentages of income spent by textile workers and their families for various purposes. For purposes of comparison The Statistical Abstract of the United States (Washington, D.C.: U.S. Bureau of the Census, 1980) gives the following percentage distribution of expenditures for personal consumption for 1979:

Food, beverage and tobacco	21.3
Clothing, accessories and jewelry	7.8
Personal care	1.3
Housing	16.0
Household operations	14.5
Medical care expenses	9.7
Personal business	5.4
Transportation	14.1
Recreation	6.7
Other	3.2

It is apparent that these data are not fully comparable with the information given in tables 3.1 and 3.3. The categories employed for 1979 differ from those used in tables 3.1 and 3.3, and the information for 1979 is based upon total expenditures rather than total income as in tables 3.1 and 3.3. (It is worth asking how much difference the latter discrepancy actually makes.)

Even so, suggestive comparisons are possible. We can see, for example, that in 1979 approximately 21 percent of expenditures went to purchase food, tobacco, and beverages, including alcoholic beverages. In contrast, textile workers and their families spent approximately 42 percent of income on food alone (table 3.1). Even families in the highest income quartile spent 39 percent of their income on food (table 3.3). In other words, the families of the late 1880s spent a larger percentage of income on food alone than was spent for food and other commodities in 1979. Similarly, in 1979 a smaller proportion of expenditures went to purchase clothing, accessories and jewelry combined than was spent for clothing alone by the families of the late 1880s. On the other hand, the burdens upon income of housing (the combined categories of housing and household operations) and medical care were apparently greater in 1979 than in the late 1880s.

Limited though they are, these comparisons suggest that the burdens of basic necessities—clothing, housing and particularly food—upon income were larger among textile workers and their families than in 1979, suggesting in turn lower standards of living. The comparisons might also be taken as suggesting other differences in living conditions and requirements. As an example, the data for the textile workers does not include a category for transportation costs.

A second set of comparisons concerns specific regional and nationality groups of textile workers and their families included in our data collection. If we assume that variations in income provide a reasonably accurate prediction of variations in living standards, expectations can be formulated concerning differences in living standards between particular regional and nationality groups. Table 2.8B above indicates that among the specific regional and nationality groups considered, the Irish families had the highest mean total family income (approximately $764 per year) and that a larger percentage of the Irish families (38 percent) ranked in the highest family income quartile. The Irish were followed by the Northern French Canadian families. They had a mean income of approximately $750, and some 35 percent of these families ranked in the highest income quartile. The French Canadians were followed by the British and Canadian families who, in turn, were followed by the Continental European families. The three native-stock groups rank lower using these measures (table 2.6).

Still assuming the rough equivalence between income and living standards, we would expect that Irish, Canadian and British families would have the highest standards of living followed in approximate order by the French Canadians, Continental Europeans, Border state native stock, Northern native stock, and the Southern native stock. Also assuming the validity of the percentage of income spent on food and end-of-year family surpluses and deficits as indicators of family living standards, we would expect that these groups of families would rank in roughly the same order in terms of these two indicators.

Tables 3.6 and 3.7 provide a test of these assumptions. Table 3.6 cross-tabulates the eight regional and nationality groups of families against the quartile distribution of percentage of family income spent on food (the quartile ranges are the same as those in table 3.5). Also given in the table is the mean percentage of income spent on food by each category of families. Table 3.7 provides the same information for the quartile distribution of family end-of-year surpluses and deficits calculated as percentages of total family income (the quartile ranges are those used in table 3.4).

In fact, neither table 3.6 nor table 3.7 suggests the expected ordering. The groups of families that ranked highest in terms of total family income do not rank highest in terms of their end-of-year financial situations or lowest in percentage of income spent on food as was naively expected. Conversely, the groups of families that appeared lowest in total family income do not appear worst off in terms of their end-of-year financial situation nor do they consistently rank highest in percentage of income spent on food. If anything, the rankings suggested by tables 3.6 and 7 are almost the reverse of those predicted on the basis of income levels. We must ask why the predicted ordering fails to appear, or, perhaps more accurately, why total family income falls so far short of adequately predicting family living conditions.

Various possible explanations will come to mind. One would be that the two variables employed in tables 3.6 and 3.7 are simply not valid indicators of living conditions. Two further questions then follow. In what specific ways are the two variables unsatisfactory? A second explanation was alluded to in this chapter. Family income is related to family living conditions, but a variety of other factors mediate that relation. The next question is, what are those mediating factors and how can they be taken into account?

One such factor might involve family tastes and values. Some families prefer, we might argue, to spend disproportionate amounts of income on things other than improvement of living conditions. Some families preferred to spend for nonmaterial things, and some chose to spend for luxuries. The consequence in both cases was that their material standard of living suffered, or so it might be argued.

We can subject this explanation to a partial test. To do so, table 3.8 cross-tabulates the percentage of family income spent for discretionary purposes, for religion, and for intoxicating beverages against the eight regional and nationality categories of families (the definition of discretionary expenditures is the same as in tables 3.1 through 3.3 above). Table 3.8 suggests that

Table 3.6
Quartile Distribution of Percent of Income Spent on Food by Place of Residence and Specific Nationality

Percentage of Families Whose Food Expenditure (Calculated as Percent of Total Income) Is In:

	First Quartile (8.59% - 36.29%)	Second Quartile (36.32% - 43.54%)	Third Quartile (43.56% - 50.77%)	Fourth Quartile (50.79% - 149.36%)	Mean Percentage of Income Spent on Food	Number of Families
Native Stock Living in the North	35.9%	27.2%	18.8%	18.0%	40.8%	749
French Canadian Living in the North	11.1	19.9	27.0	42.0	49.3	226
Canadian Living in the North	13.5	12.5	21.9	52.1	52.7	96
British Living in the North	29.1	25.1	28.0	17.8	41.9	443
Irish Living in the North	17.9	22.8	25.4	33.8	47.3	464
Continental European Living in the North	29.9	24.0	23.1	23.1	43.7	221
Native Stock Living in Border States	18.5	22.3	31.1	28.2	46.0	238
Native Stock Living in South	21.1	29.8	27.7	21.4	43.6	574

This table does not include the 32 foreign-stock families residing in the Border and Southern States.

discretionary spending, calculated as percentages of total family income, did not vary greatly from one group of families to the other. On the other hand, spending for religious purposes and for intoxicating liquors varied rather widely from one group to the next. The question we must address, however,

Table 3.7
Quartile Distribution of Family End-of-Year Surpluses and Deficits as Percentages of Total Income by Regional and Nationality Groups

Percentage of Families With End-of-Year Surpluses and Deficits in:

	First Quartile	Second Quartile	Third Quartile	Fourth Quartile	Number of Families
Northern Native Stock	19.6%	21.6%	28.2%	30.6%	749
Northern French Canadian	23.0	27.0	23.9	26.1	226
Northern Canadian	40.6	30.2	15.6	13.5	96
Northern British	21.7	22.8	23.3	32.3	443
Northern Irish	30.2	22.4	22.2	25.2	464
Northern Continental European	22.2	24.4	22.6	30.8	221
Border State Native Stock	23.9	24.8	29.8	21.4	238
Southern Native Stock	30.0	32.2	25.3	12.5	574

Table 3.8
Expenditures for Discretionary Purposes, Religious Expenses, and Intoxicating Liquors by Regional and Nationality Groups

	Mean Percentage of Income Spent for Discretionary Purposes	Mean Annual Expenditure for Religion	Mean Annual Expenditures for Intoxicating Liquors
Northern Native Stock	6.0%	$5.16	$3.51
Northern French Canadian	6.0	13.74	6.87
Northern Canadian	6.7	13.58	8.11
Northern British	6.6	7.91	6.76
Northern Irish	6.8	14.02	7.46
Northern Continental European	7.1	7.68	10.70
Border State Native Stock	4.7	3.64	1.27
Southern Native Stock	5.9	4.55	3.08

is whether the table suggests that spending for these purposes could have accounted for the mismatch between total family income and the ordering of groups of families in terms of living conditions that appears in tables 3.6 and 3.7. Is it likely that variations in spending for the purposes given in table 3.8—or for other discretionary purposes—could account for the differences in living conditions suggested by tables 3.6 and 7? How likely is it that the families suffered poor living conditions because they chose to spend large amounts for discretionary purposes?

— 4 —
FAMILY COMPOSITION
AND STRUCTURE

Researchers have devoted considerable time and energy to investigating the size and composition of families in diverse historical contexts. Differences in family characteristics and practices have been observed both from one time period to another and from one cultural or nationality group to the next. Differences include variations in the size of families, the age of parents at marriage and their age when first children were born, the age of children when they left home, and many other family characteristics.

A variety of factors have been seen as causing such differences. Religious tenets and affiliations are sometimes seen as leading some groups to have larger numbers of children and to follow different family practices. There is indication that in some cultures a large number of children was seen as a mark of masculine virility. In some historical periods and economic settings children were seen as additional sources of family income and of support when parents reached old age. In other settings, children were seen as added burdens upon the earning power of parents. Hence parents differed in their interest in having children.

For a number of reasons, then, we can expect that among the textile workers of concern here more or less predictable differences in family characteristics will appear. Such expectations and questions are of intrinsic interest, but chapter 2 suggests further expectations and questions that are of equal interest. In that chapter it appeared that the Northern foreign stock had more sources of income, particularly working children, than Northern native-stock families. As a consequence, we might expect to find that some nationality groups among the Northern foreign stock also included more, and more older, children. Still a further inference would be that the parents in these families tended to be older since parents with older children tend to be older than parents with younger children.

These expected differences in family size and the age of children and parents do not follow necessarily from the examination in chapter 2. We might find that large numbers of working children among the Northern foreign stock had nothing to do with differences in family size. The Northern foreign stock may have more frequently sent children to work rather than to school and the opposite tendency may have been present among the Northern native stock. If so, we would find that families in the two groups did not differ either in number of children or in the age of parents or children. If the size and age distribution of the two groups of families proved similar, then the combination of evidence might suggest differences in family needs, preferences, and practices in sending children to work or school.

To emphasize a point, we are concerned here not only with the size, number of children, and other objective characteristics of families but also with developing inferences bearing upon more complex issues, including differences in family practices and values. We would like to formulate plausible explanations for differences in the size and other characteristics of families. For these purposes our source material has both strengths and ambiguities.

FAMILY AND HOUSEHOLD SIZE

At first glance, constructing a description of the size and structure of the families seems a rather uncomplicated and straightforward matter. In fact, however, even this simple task requires meticulous care in interpreting the data and in defining seemingly obvious terms. The resulting description, moreover, rests upon several assumptions.

We can quite readily identify some characteristics of the families. In the large majority of households both a husband and wife were present. Only 195 households included no husband and only 87 no wife. The households ranged in size from one with a single member and 227 with two members to two with 22 members. While some households were quite large and others quite small, median household size was 4.6 members; approximately eighty-nine percent of the households included eight or fewer members; and about 70 percent included six or fewer. Nationality and regional groups differed in household size. The Northern native-stock households were smallest, with a median of 3.9 members as compared to 5.0 members for the Northern foreign stock, 5.5 for the Border State native stock, and 4.7 for the Southern native stock.

Unfortunately, accurate measurement of family size is more complicated. The preceding discussion refers to households rather than families. The distinction reflects both ambiguities of the data and variations in living arrangements. Households and families are not the same thing. Some households reflected in the source collection included "boarders and others." Boarders were apparently not related to the families but contributed to family income. Differences in household size, therefore, are not reliable indications of differences in family size. One implication is that the Northern native-stock families actually may not have been smaller than Northern foreign-stock families, even though household sizes differed. More households in the other groups may have included boarders and others.

We must therefore examine the composition of the households more closely. A total of 983 households included boarders and others; 2,060 did not. Only about 21 percent of the Northern native-stock households included such individuals as compared to 33 percent of the Northern foreign-stock households, 42 percent of the Border State native stock, and 42 percent of the Southern native-stock. Thus it is possible that Northern native-stock families, as opposed to households, were in fact no smaller than families in the other regional and national groups.

The information on boarders and others is also ambiguous. In the first place, the meaning of the word "boarder" is unclear. A strict definition would treat these individuals as taking some or all of their meals ("boarding") with the families but not residing, or "rooming," with them. In practice, however, the two terms were often used interchangeably. The data also provide no information about the "others" that are reported as included in the households. However, data on income provided by the collection indicates that of the 983 households with "boarders and others" only 729 reported income from boarders.

We could plausibly infer that these "other" individuals who apparently did not pay board were, in effect, members of the families, but were neither a husband, a wife, nor one of the children of the family. Some households undoubtedly included relatives—grandparents, grandchildren, or the wife or husband of an older child—who resided with the families on a more-or-less continuing basis. It may well be that in some cases unrelated individuals lived with the families. Such arrangements occur today, and sometimes constitute a means by which unattached individuals are provided a home, or by which individuals who are unable to care for themselves—the aged or orphans, for example—are supported and cared for. It is even possible that some of the "others" were "live-in" servants of one sort or the other.

Table 4.1 attempts to reduce these ambiguities by presenting "corrected" family size for the same four regional and nationality groups as in table 3.4. For the table it is assumed that non-paying boarders and others in the households were effectively members of the families and these individuals are included in the table. To eliminate ambiguities produced by paying boarders, all families that reported income from boarders are excluded from the tabulation. This "corrected" estimate of family size takes into account the presence of unidentified "others" in households that did not include paying boarders.

Using this corrected estimate, Northern native-stock families still appear smaller than the other regional and nationality groups. Median family size for the Northern native stock is 3.7 members; for the Northern foreign stock, 4.5; 4.6 for the Border state native stock; and 4.4 for the Southern native stock.

The tendency of Northern native-stock families to be smaller is apparent

Table 4.1
"Corrected" Family Size by Place of Residence and Nationality*

Number of Family Members	Northern Native Stock	Northern Foreign Stock	Border State Native Stock	Southern Native Stock	All Families
1	0.0%	0.0%	0.0%	0.2%	0.0%
2	13.0	8.2	7.8	10.0	9.9
3	20.9	14.7	20.8	16.9	17.2
4	22.8	19.0	12.3	15.7	19.0
5	19.8	15.4	15.6	19.6	17.4
6	11.8	13.8	11.7	10.3	12.5
7	6.5	10.0	16.9	12.3	9.9
8	2.9	7.7	8.4	6.9	6.2
9	1.5	4.4	2.6	5.6	3.7
10	0.2	4.2	1.9	1.5	2.4
11	0.5	1.3	1.3	0.5	0.9
12	0.2	0.8	0.6	0.2	0.5
13 or more	0.0	0.5	0.0	0.2	0.3
Total	100.0%	100.0%	100.0%	100.0%	100.0%

*Family size, as calculated for this Table, includes non-paying Boarders but excludes paying boarders, and does not include the 32 foreign-stock families residing in the Border and Southern states.

in table 4.1. A somewhat larger percentage of the Northern native-stock included only two members as compared with smaller percentages for the other groups. Summing down the columns of the table we can see that approximately 57 percent of the Northern native-stock families included four or fewer members as compared with 42 percent of the Northern foreign stock, 41 percent of the Border State native stock, and 43 percent of the Southern native stock. Only about five percent of the Northern native-stock included eight or more members, while some 19 percent of the Northern foreign-stock, 15 percent of the Border State native-stock, and 15 percent of the Southern native-stock families included eight or more members.

We can also see differences in family size by comparing the number of children for the four groups. Given in the rows of the table 4.2 are the percentages of families in each group with given numbers of children. Summing down the columns we see that approximately 59 percent of the Northern native-stock families included two or fewer children as compared with 44 percent of the Northern foreign-stock families, 36 percent of the Border State native stock and 45 percent of the Southern native stock. In the same way we can also see that only about 11 percent of the Northern native-stock families included five or more children as compared with 28

Table 4.2
Number of Children in Families by Place of Residence and Nationality *

	Percentage of Specific Group with Number of Children:				
Number of Children	Northern Native-Stock	Northern Foreign-Stock	Border State Native-Stock	Southern Native-Stock	All Families
0	15.0%	9.7%	8.0%	11.0%	11.1%
1	21.9	14.7	14.3	18.6	17.2
2	22.3	19.3	14.3	15.5	18.9
3	19.5	16.3	18.1	18.8	17.7
4	10.5	12.5	15.5	10.3	11.8
5 or more	10.8	27.6	29.8	25.8	23.2
Total	100.0%	100.1%	100.0%	100.0%	99.9%

* This table does not include the 32 foreign-stock families residing in the Border and Southern states.

percent of the Northern foreign stock, 30 percent of the Border State native stock, and 23 percent of the Southern native stock.

It is clear that the four regional and nationality groups differed in the size of families. We can also draw further conclusions. Most of the families were "nuclear" in nature in that they included only two generations, fathers and mothers and their children. A small number (254, or about eight percent) may have been "extended" in structure, in that they may have included other relatives in addition to parents and their children. It is possible, as well, that some of the households that included paying boarders also included other relatives. While most families were nuclear, residence with families of unrelated individuals was relatively common. Almost a quarter of the families reported income from boarders. Generalizations on this score, however, are conditional upon ambiguities concerning the meaning of the "boarders and others" category.

AGE

Differences in the number of children between the several nationality and regional groups lead us to inferences concerning differences in the ages of family members. It is possible for older people to have greater numbers of children than younger people; the older people are, the greater the likelihood that they will have larger numbers of children; and larger families are likely to include more older children than smaller families. Thus we can expect to find that differences in age between groups will appear in association with differences in family size.

Comparison of the median ages of the husbands in the four regional and nationality groups confirms these inferences. The median age of all husbands in the entire group of families is 39.4 years. As we expected on the basis of family size, the Northern native-stock husbands appear youngest with a median age of 35.3 years, and the Southern native-stock appear next youngest with a median of 39.3 years. In contrast, and as we also expected, the Border State native-stock and the Northern foreign-stock husbands appear older with median ages of 42.5 and 41.6 years, respectively.

We can gain a more precise view of age differences by looking at the age distribution of husbands. Selecting age fifty arbitrarily, it appears that only 12 percent of the Northern native-stock husbands were fifty or older as compared with approximately 27 percent of the Northern foreign-stock husbands, 29 percent of the Border State native stock, and 23 percent of the Southern native stock. Clearly the age differences we expected do appear. (We should ask ourselves why Northern native-stock husbands tended to be younger than husbands in other regional and nationality groups.)

These differences in the ages of husbands lead us to expect even more strongly that children also differed in age. Unfortunately, in examining of these differences we confront additional difficulties. Table 4.3 presents for each of the groups of families the median age of children for each of eight birth order categories. The table gives median age for the oldest children in the families, the median age for the next oldest children, and so on. The birth order categories necessarily refer only to living children that still resided with their parents. An unknown number of additional children had either died, moved away from the family, or would be born at a later time.

Table 4.3 provides a number of items of information. As we see, the median age of children declines moving from the oldest to the eighth-oldest category. As we would expect, the latter-born children tended to be younger and more similar in age than the earlier-born children. As we also expected, the table reflects the younger age of Northern native-stock families. The median age of Northern native-stock children tends to be lower in each birth order category than that of the other regional and nationality groups except for the oldest category. The number of children in the two oldest birth order categories is small, and the age medians for these categories, as a consequence, are less meaningful.

Table 4.3
Median Age of Children in Each Birth Order Category
by Place of Residence and Nationality *

Birth Order of Children	Median Age of Children (in years):				
	Northern Native-Stock	Northern Foreign-Stock	Border State Native-Stock	Southern Native-Stock	All Families
First	9.1	15.0	16.3	15.1	13.8
Second	7.1	12.9	13.6	13.0	11.7
Third	5.6	11.1	11.3	11.1	9.9
Fourth	5.0	9.1	8.9	8.9	8.2
Fifth	4.3	7.4	6.9	6.2	6.6
Sixth	4.2	6.2	4.3	5.3	5.5
Seventh	4.2	4.5	3.3	4.1	4.3
Eighth	4.0	2.9	2.0	3.7	3.2

* This table does not include the 32 foreign-stock families residing in the Border and Southern states.

FAMILY PRACTICES

Differences in the age of husbands and children in the several groups are in accord with the differences in family size and in the number of children in families that we observed above. These age differences are also in keeping with the differences in the incidence of working children seen in chapter 2. The next question is, can we use differences of this sort to infer differences in family practices, values, and preferences? Can we plausibly infer, for example, that some groups valued larger numbers of children and also preferred that children remain at home, perhaps as means to augment family income? The answer is that we can draw some plausible inferences of this sort but we will be unable to establish them with certainty.

We can establish that the regional and nationality groups differed in the number of older children still residing at home. Among the children in Northern native-stock families, for example, only approximately eight percent were eighteen or older. The comparable figures for the other groups are notably higher: 18 percent among the Northern foreign stock and the Border State native stock, and 15 percent among the Southern native-stock families. We can also establish that the latter groups included more working children. Approximately 15 percent of the children in Northern native-stock families were reported as employed, as compared to 34 percent among the Northern foreign-stock children, almost 43 percent of the Border State native stock, and almost 50 percent for the Southern native stock.

On the basis of these differences we can obviously infer that working was not confined to older children. Clearly, children under eighteen were frequently employed. Can we also infer that Northern native-stock children tended to leave home at a younger age than children in other groups, reflecting differences in family practices and preferences? Similarly, can we infer on the basis of differences in number of children that foreign-stock families in the North, for whatever reasons, preferred larger numbers of children than Northern native-stock families? The differences observed above are compatible with these inferences but neither demonstrate them nor rule out other possibilities.

The difficulty is twofold. One problem is differences in age between parents in the several groups; the second is the "cross-sectional" nature of the data collection. The Northern native-stock textile workers and their families are younger than the other groups. It is possible that the sample of families is biased in this respect. Somehow in selecting families to be interviewed, the officials inadvertently selected a disproportionate number of younger native-stock families in the North. It is also possible that Northern native-stock textile workers and their families actually did tend to be younger than other groups. In this case, the sample is not biased but accurately represents the actual age differences between the groups.

In either case, our problem remains. For whatever reason, husbands in Northern native-stock families included in the collection did tend to be younger. We would expect that families with younger husbands would tend to be smaller with more younger children, and we would expect the obverse of families with older husbands. In other words, differences in the size of families and the age of children are explicable on grounds other than differences in preferences and family practices.

The problem is compounded by the cross-sectional nature of the data collection. The data were collected at a single time point and give us a glimpse of the families as they existed at that time. The data do not allow us to follow the families through time and see the changes that they would undergo. If the same families had been interviewed at a later time it is possible that no differences would appear between the Northern native stock and the other groups. As the Northern native stock aged, their children would also age, perhaps remain at home, and additional children might be born, so that these families would come to resemble the other groups. There is no necessary reason to believe that the differences between the groups would be eradicated as the Northern native-stock families aged, but nothing in the data rules the possibility out.

We can employ two approaches, and others are possible, to reduce these inferential difficulties and improve our ability to draw plausible inferences concerning family practices and preferences. One involves controlling on the age of parents. As we noted, the appearance that the Northern native

Table 4.4
Families with Three or More Children by Husband's Age,
Place of Residence, and Nationality

Percentage of Families with Three or More Children:

Husband's Age	Northern Native Stock	Northern Foreign Stock	Border State Native Stock	Southern Native Stock	All Families
18-27	7.7%	16.0%	9.4%	8.0%	11.0%
28-37	41.5	50.7	49.0	50.0	47.1
38-47	56.5	74.0	90.8	78.2	71.7
48-57	40.0	64.1	81.8	71.7	63.3
58-67	23.8	35.8	52.4	55.2	39.3

* This table does not include the 32 foreign-stock families residing in the Border and Southern states.

stock had fewer children than families in other regional and nationality groups could be due to the younger age of the Northern native-stock parents. If so, differences in number of children between the Northern native stock and the other groups would disappear when the age of parents is held constant. That is, if the groups did not differ in family practices, parents in the same age category ought to have approximately the same number of children regardless of nationality or region of residence.

Table 4.4 tests this possibility by grouping the families in terms of the ages of husbands. Families with husbands ranging from eighteen through twenty-seven are grouped in the first age category, those with husbands in the age range twenty-eight through thirty-seven in the second age category, and so on. The number of families with husbands of sixty-eight years of age or greater is too small to be considered. The cell entries in the table are the percentages of families in each group that included three or more children. Again, if the appearance of fewer children among the Northern native stock was simply a reflection of the younger age of native-stock parents, the cell entries for each age category would be approximately the same for the four regional and nationality groups.

We do not find this distribution. In each age category the percentage of Northern native-stock families with three or more children is smaller than in the case of the other groups. The only exception is the Southern native-stock families in the youngest age category. It will be noted, of course, that the analysis presented in table 4.4 is relatively crude. The age categories employed are quite broad, and combining families with three or more children into a single category undoubtedly masks variation. It may be, therefore, that more detailed categories would reveal additional differences.

Even so, we can now argue with greater confidence that the smaller number of children among Northern native-stock families was independent of differences in the age of parents. This finding is compatible with the notion that Northern native-stock parents preferred fewer children. In contrast, parents in other regional and nationality groups may have placed greater value on larger numbers of children. A second approach provides a further test of this inference.

Parents that place value upon larger numbers of children, or feel obligated to have children, would probably tend to marry earlier and have children at earlier ages than parents that do not share these views. Thus the age of parents at the birth of the first child might be taken as an indicator of attitudes toward child bearing. It is superficially easy to estimate the age of mothers in the textile workers' families at the birth of their first child by subtracting the age of the eldest child in the household from the age of the mother. When these operations are carried out, however, difficulties become immediately apparent.

When we use these calculations, it appears that mothers ranged at the birth of their first child from five to thirty-five years of age-not a fully sensible result. In terms of the calculations, however, only approximately three percent of the mothers were fourteen or younger at the birth of the eldest child residing with the families. We can surmise, therefore, that some of these mothers were stepmothers and that the appearance of very early ages at birth of first children is a reflection of second or, for that matter, subsequent marriages.

The opposite end of the age spectrum also presents a difficulty. The data collection gives only the age of the eldest children still residing with the families. It does not give the age of the oldest child "ever born" to families. It is likely that in some families older children had already left home or had died and the estimates really reflect the age of mothers at the birth of a second, third, or subsequent child. Only about ten percent of the mothers included in the data collection were, according to the calculations, over twenty-five at the birth of the eldest child residing with the families.

We can reduce, but not eliminate, these difficulties by constraining the age ranges employed. Table 4.5 (p. 78) presents the age of mothers at the birth of the oldest child still residing with the families. Only mothers who appear as of fifteen through thirty years of age at the birth of the eldest child are included. Since only ten percent of the mothers were between twenty-six and thirty at the birth of the eldest child, this group is combined into a single category.

The table is complex and the differences relatively small. A little summing down the columns reduces complexity and summarizes the data. When that is done we find that only about 24 percent of the Northern native-stock mothers were twenty years of age or less at the birth of the eldest child still residing with the family. In contrast, approximately 33 percent of the Northern foreign-stock mothers, 44 percent of the Border State native-stock mothers, and 54 percent of the Southern native-stock mothers were twenty or younger at the birth of the eldest child residing with the families. By examining the table closely, moreover, we can see that the specific age categories are almost consistently marked by similar differences.

The table suggests, then, that the Northern native stock tended to marry and have children at somewhat older ages than did the other groups. The Northern foreign stock, so it would appear, tended to marry and have children somewhat later than did either the Border State or Southern native stock, although the differences are not entirely consistent. Apparently, the Southern native-stock tended to marry and have children at earlier ages than did the other groups. (These differences might, in turn, provide a basis for inferences about differences in attitudes toward child bearing. It should be kept in mind that the data do present difficulties and the degree of confidence with which generalization can be made and inferences drawn should be carefully considered.)

GENERALIZATIONS

By now we are probably willing to conclude that the several regional and nationality groups differed in family practices and preferences. The various steps in our analysis make it unlikely that differences in family size and in the number and age of children were merely the artificial products of the sample or other flaws in the data or our interpretations.

We might also be inclined to conclude that these differences can be explained by religious difference or economic considerations, to name only

Table 4.5
Age of Mothers at Birth of Oldest Child Still
Residing with the Family, by Place of Residence and Nationality *

Age of Mother at Birth of Oldest Child	Percentage of Families with Mother's Age at Birth of Oldest Child:				
	Northern Native Stock	Northern Foreign Stock	Border State Native Stock	Southern Native Stock	All Families
15	0.8%	2.0%	1.6%	2.9%	1.7%
16	1.0	2.5	0.0	5.1	2.3
17	1.6	2.9	4.9	9.1	3.6
18	3.4	6.5	3.3	10.9	5.9
19	7.1	7.4	14.8	12.0	8.5
20	9.9	11.2	19.7	14.3	11.7
21	16.8	13.0	14.8	14.3	14.7
22	19.9	13.5	8.2	9.1	14.8
23	13.6	10.8	8.2	5.1	10.7
24	10.7	11.7	4.9	6.9	10.2
25	6.0	6.5	11.5	12.9	6.0
26-30	9.1	12.1	3.3	2.3	10.0

* This table does not include the 32 foreign-stock families residing in the Border and Southern states.

two possible explanations. While these explanations are certainly plausible and highly interesting, we will recognize that they are not based upon the data; they depend upon other sources.

The examination also illustrates a more general and in some respects more important point. Questions of family size, age, and numbers of children seem quite straightforward, and comparison of groups of families in terms of these characteristics seems at first glance a simple matter. It turns out, however, that despite the rich and detailed nature of the data collection, these family characteristics are not as direct or clear cut as they first seem. As we move from the objective characteristics of families—size, age, and numbers of children—to such matters as attitudes toward childbearing, difficulties are obviously compounded.

TO THE READER

Differences in the size and structure of families between regional and national groups are of interest in their own right. As will be recognized, these comparisons are also relevant to assessing and explaining differences in living conditions from one group of families to the next. They are relevant as well to developing and testing inferences concerning differences in family practices among the several groups.

As it turned out, these comparisons proved to be less straightforward and more problematic than they initially seemed. One problem is the presence of paying boarders and other unidentified individuals among the families. A second and in some degree more difficult problem is the cross-sectional nature of the data. The data provide a view of the families at the time of interview, but do not provide information bearing upon the history or future of the families.

To partially cope with these difficulties we extended our examination by attempting to assess the age of mothers at the birth of the eldest child still residing with the families. Our argument was that if particular groups tended to prefer larger numbers of children, placed greater value upon family life, saw children as economic advantages, or felt obligated for whatever reason to have larger numbers of children, the members of those groups would tend to marry and have children at an earlier age than did members of groups who did not fully share these preferences, values, or senses of need or obligation.

In fact we did find differences between the several groups in terms of age of mothers at the birth of eldest children. To make these comparisons we required a number of assumptions but the differences that appeared were in keeping with differences in family size and in number of children seen in earlier tables. When we compared the number of children in families controlling on the age of husbands (table 4.4), we found similar differences which lent additional credibility to the examination.

In some ways, table 4.5 is the most interesting table in the chapter since it seems intuitively to bear most directly upon differences in marital and child-bearing practices and values. This examination, however, confronts difficulties in addition to those summarized above. For one thing, the data report age in whole years. This means that an individual reported, for example, as twenty-four years old could have ranged (in principle) anywhere from twenty-four years and one day of age to twenty-four years and 364 days. The further consequence is that our estimates of the age of women at the birth of the eldest child are unavoidably imprecise.

A second problem is the likelihood that the ages reported in the data collection are sometimes erroneous. Obviously, the data provided no direct indication of the incidence or magnitude of inaccuracies but indirect indications can be developed. We would expect, for example, that the wives reflected in the collection would be randomly distributed in terms of age. Within limits, we would expect that roughly the same number of wives would be of each age. We would not expect that the age distribution would systematically "heap" at particular ages, such as ages ending in zero and five. In fact, heaping at ages ending in zero or five is usually taken as an indication of inaccuracy; people who do not know, cannot recall, or are unwilling to give their correct age tend to round their age to numbers ending in zero or five.

The data for French Canadian women (the French Canadians are selected arbitrarily) provide some indication of age heaping and hence of inaccuracy (table 4.6). As we see, twelve of these women are reported as of age twenty-five but only seven and six, respectively, as of age twenty-four and twenty-six; twelve are reported as thirty but only six and nine as of twenty-nine and thirty-one; and other examples of heaping can also be seen.

The point is that the differences observed in table 4.5 can be challenged on two grounds: the manner in which age is recorded and evidence of inaccuracies in the ages reported. The question follows, is it likely that these considerations could account for the differences that appear in table 4.5? Should these differences be dismissed on the grounds that they are really the product of limitations of the data rather than indications of actual differences between the several groups?

The same reasoning that underlies table 4.5 suggests a further test of the view that the nationality and regional groups differed in systematic ways in their attitudes toward child-bearing, marriage, and the family. If the groups differed in desire for children, contraceptive practices, and the like, it might be expected that they would also differ in the time intervals between the birth of children. The interval between children would tend to be shorter among those groups that preferred larger families than among those that did not share that preference. These comparisons could be carried out in reasonably straightforward fashion. The question is, would this comparison be useful in view of the characteristics of the data noted above? (In considering this question, thought should be given to the length of the human gestation period.)

The discussion in the body of this chapter compares four regional and nationality groups; variation within these groups is masked. Information bearing upon the family characteristics of specific groups would be desirable. Is it now possible on the basis of the final sections of chapters 2 and 3 to make predictions concerning what would be found if the size and other characteristics of the eight more specific nationality groups considered in those sections were examined in detail?

As an example, does the information provided by tables 3.6 and 3.7 give us a basis for predicting differences in the size of families or in the age of children and parents between the eight regional and nationality groups? Would we be willing to predict that groups of families that appear relatively worse off in terms of the indicators of living conditions used in those tables

Table 4.6
Number of French Canadian Wives by Reported Year of Age

Age (in years)	Number of Wives	Age (in years)	Number of Wives	Age (in years)	Number of Wives
18	1	32	8	46	18
19	1	33	9	47	5
20	2	34	7	48	10
21	2	35	5	49	1
22	4	36	5	50	7
23	4	37	7	52	3
24	7	38	7	52	3
25	12	39	2	53	2
26	6	40	16	55	
27	8	41	6	59	3
28	9	42	6		
29	6	43	4		
30	12	44	5		
31	9	45	10		

would also tend to include more children, older children, and older parents than the groups that appeared relatively better off in terms of those indicators? Perhaps not. We also know that the groups of families varied in income levels, and we would not be willing to assume that levels of income were entirely irrelevant to family living conditions.

Alternatively, then, does the combination of tables 3.6 and 3.7 and tables 2.9A and 2.9B which bear upon total family income aid in predicting differences in family size between the several groups? Would we expect that families that ranked relatively high in terms of total income but relatively worse off in living conditions would tend to have larger numbers of children? What about families that ranked relatively poorly in total income but appeared relatively well off in terms of the indicators of living conditions? Would the same predictions apply to the age of children? Would families that ranked high in total income but low in terms of living conditions tend to include more older children? How about the age of parents? Would parents tend to be older in groups of families with high total incomes but poor living conditions?

Partial evaluation of these and related predictions can be carried out using the information provided by table 4.7. That table gives for each of the eight regional and nationality groups the median age of husbands and eldest children along with the median number of children. The question is, to what degree does this information confirm or refute predictions such as those in the preceding paragraphs? In what ways is that information limited and misleading in terms of these predictions?

Table 4.7
Median Age of Husbands and Eldest Children and
Median Number of Children for Regional and Nationality Groups

	Median Age of Husbands	Median Age of Eldest Child	Median Number of Children
Northern Native Stock	35.3	9.1	1.6
Northern French Canadian	38.4	14.0	3.0
Northern Canadian	39.0	15.1	3.3
Northern British	41.4	14.1	1.9
Northern Irish	44.6	17.4	2.7
Northern Continental European	39.7	12.6	2.0
Border State Native Stock	42.5	16.3	2.7
Southern Native Stock	39.3	15.1	2.3

ILLUSTRATIONS

84

Women's Clothing Advertisement.   SOURCE: Fred L. Israel, ed. *1897 Sears Roebuck Catalog* (Reprint: New York: Chelsea House, 1968), p. 270.

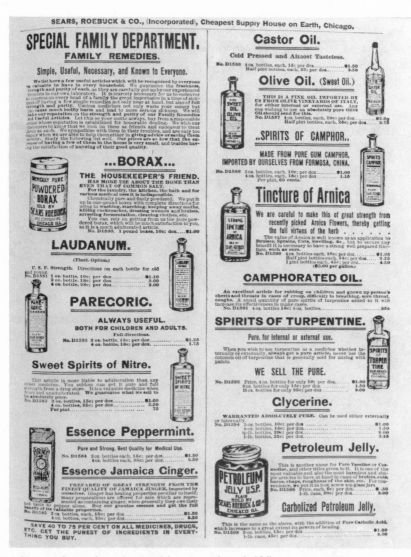

Family Remedies and articles "useful in every household." SOURCE: *1897 Sears Roebuck Catalog*, "Drug Department" insert.

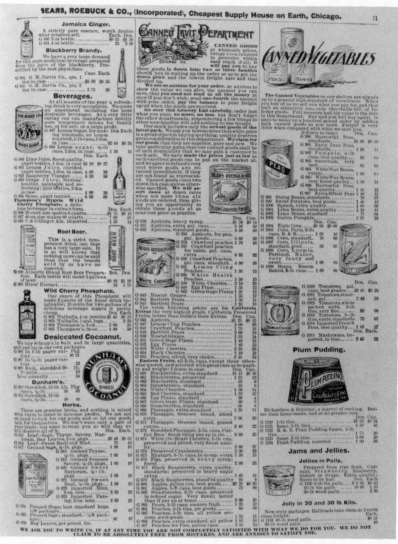

Canned, bottled, and otherwise preserved food and beverage items available via mail order. SOURCE: *1897 Sears Roebuck Catalog*, p. 11.

Clothes for women and children.   SOURCE: *1897 Sears Roebuck Catalog*, p. 242.

Men's work clothes advertisements stressed durability. SOURCE: *1897 Sears Roebuck Catalog*, p. 178.

SEARS, ROEBUCK & CO., (Incorporated), Cheapest Supply House on Earth, Chicago.

NUMBER 104

Sears, Roebuck and Co. — Incorporated — Cheapest Supply House on Earth — Our Trade Reaches Around the World — Consumers Guide

THE POLICY OF OUR HOUSE

It is the Policy of Our House to Supply the Consumer Everything on which we can save him money. goods that can be delivered at your door anywhere in the United States for less than they can be procured from your local dealer; and although our line covers about everything the consumer uses, there is scarcely an article but what will admit of a saving of at least 15%, and from that to 75%, to say nothing of the fact that our goods are as a rule of a higher grade than those carried by the average retailer or catalogue house, and we earnestly believe a careful comparison will convince you that we can furnish you more and better goods for your dollar than you can obtain from any other establishment in the United States.

We Aim to Illustrate Honestly and Correctly Every Article. So far as possible, illustrations are engraved from photographs taken directly from the article. Our illustrations and descriptions are such as will enable you to order intelligently, in fact, so that you can tell what you are getting as well as if you were in our store selecting the goods from stock.

We Employ No Agents. By the aid of our numerous catalogues our customers can deal with us direct. Thus the Farmer, Miner, Mechanic, Business Man, in fact anyone, can send in his or her own order and save money.

Our Terms are Alike to All.

Our Employees are Instructed to Treat Every Customer at a Distance Exactly as They Would Like to be Treated were they in the customer's place, in fact, if you favor us with your patronage we will feel under obligations to do everything in our power to merit your trade, and no matter how small your order may be it will receive the same prompt and careful attention as if it were ever so large.

We Aim to Treat Our Customers in a manner calculated to secure their permanent patronage. The unprecedented growth of our business proves that we have succeeded in supplying the wants of the people in a satisfactory manner and at lower prices than they could possibly secure elsewhere.

We Deem that the Best Advertisement Any Firm Can Have is a well satisfied customer. We aim to bring the manufacturer and consumer closer together. The closer the relation between the manufacturer and consumer, the more economy to all concerned, and in a great measure it does away with the long chain of profits in the handling of merchandise.

We are Able by Reason of Our Enormous Output of Goods to make contracts with representative manufacturers and importers for such large quantities of merchandise that we can secure the lowest possible prices. To this we add the smallest percentage of profit possible, and through the medium of catalogues offer the goods to our customers, and on our economic one-small-profit plan, direct from manufacturer to consumer, a large percentage of the merchandise we handle is owned by the purchaser at less than local dealers can buy in quantities.

A Trial Order Will Convince You of the Saving worked by our economic one-small-profit plan. If you contemplate purchasing any article of merchandise, we would consider it a privilege to quote you our lowest price, irrespective of whether you buy from us or not. It will be a safeguard against your paying someone else too much money. It will also open up a correspondence between us, and may eventually lead to our selling you some article of merchandise for which we may be able to demonstrate the saving of our method.

WHERE WE SELL GOODS

Our Catalogues and Other Printed Matter may Fall into the Hands of those Living at Remote Distances who will not think of buying owing to the great distance. Don't think you live too far away. THERE IS NOT A TOWN IN THE UNITED STATES WHERE WE HAVE NOT SOLD GOODS. Our goods go into every city, town and hamlet in every state, as well as to almost every country on the globe. DISTANCE CUTS NO FIGURE. We can serve you at any time and in any place. Our largest trade is in Pennsylvania, next in New York, third Illinois, fourth Ohio, and so on according to the population of the different states.

Freight and Express Rates are Usually Low and we have special facilities for shipping, carefully consulting the various classifications so as to pack your goods in such a manner as will entitle them to the lowest possible transportation charges.

Get Other Information Concerning Express and Freight Rates on the following pages, and you will see that the transportation amounts to next to nothing as compared with what you save in price.

Consider You Pay Freight or Express no matter Where You Live or Where You Buy. You may as well pay it to the railroad company and be dealing direct with first hands, as to pay it in the way of an exorbitant price to local dealers.

ABOUT UNPROFITABLE SHIPMENTS.

We Not Infrequently Receive Orders which we Term "Unprofitable" Shipments. For example: A party living far distant may order a dollar's worth of sugar to go by express. The express charges would equal the cost of the sugar. We occasionally get an order for heavy hardware, the order amounting to 10 per haps less than $5.00. The goods weigh 100 pounds. We are asked to ship them by express. This is usually an unprofitable shipment. A single pair of heavy cheap boots to go a great distance by express, or of very bulky wooden ware, or furniture, or other merchandise, might be what we term an unprofitable shipment.

We Would Advise Our Customers to Study the Freight and Express Rates as given on the following pages, for we do not wish you to send us a dollar for anything unless we can save you money on the purchase.

Orders that Would Be Unprofitable to Ship by Mail or Express May Be Very Profitable When Sent by Freight, but as 100 pounds is usually carried by freight for the same charge as 10 pounds, by adding other merchandise to your order, either for yourself or by getting your neighbors to join you in making up a large order, it will make the shipment very profitable.

Masthead page of 1897 Sears, Roebuck & Co. Catalog. SOURCE: *1897 Sears Roebuck Catalog*, p. 1.

90

"Workingmen's cottages—better class." Bayonne, New Jersey. SOURCE: U.S. Public Housing Administration pictorial records from the period 1895-1905. National Archives Photo no. 196-GS-539.

"Rear of typical row of houses [in Trenton, New Jersey]. $12.00-14.00 per month." SOURCE National Archives Photo no. 196-GS-539.

"Bread for sale" from street vendor [in New York City?]   SOURCE: National Archives Photo no. 196-GS-376.

"Push cart market" in New York City.   SOURCE: National Archives Photo no. 196-GS-382.

Workers at a spinning machine in the Mollhan Mill, Newberry, South Carolina, December 1908. SOURCE: Lewis Hine Collection, Library of Congress Photo no. LC-USZ62-51053. (Hereafter Hine/LC)

Wylie Mill overseer and family, Chester, South Carolina, November 1908. SOURCE: Hine/LC LC-USZ62-86260.

Children in front of Chester, South Carolina home. The three older children pictured here worked in the Wylie Mill.   SOURCE: Hine/LC LC-USZ62-55968.

Child worker climbing on spinning frame to mend broken threads and put back empty bobbin: Bibb Mill, no. 1, Macon, Georgia, January 1909.   SOURCE: Hine/LC LC-USZ62-23944.

Homes of workers in Willingham Cotton Mills, Macon, Georgia, January 1909. SOURCE: Hine/ LC Lot 7479, Photo no. 516.

Housing conditions at Roanoke Company Cotton Mills "are not very good. Houses run down and not well kept." Roanoke, Virginia, May 1911. SOURCE: Hine/LC LC-USZ62-29097.

"Flash light photo of John Sousa [a worker in a New Bedford, Massachusetts cotton mill], his mother and some brothers and sisters. Crowded, dirty home." January 1912.   SOURCE: Hine/ LC LC-USZ62-86267.

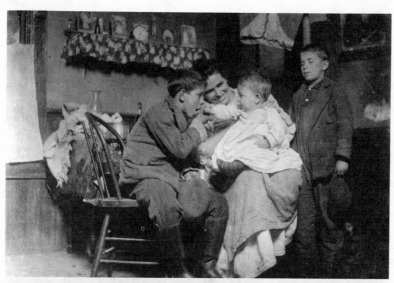

"Overcrowded home of workers in cotton mill, Providence, Rhode Island. Eight persons live in 3 small rooms, 3 of them are boarders. Inner bedrooms are 9 × 8 feet, the largest room 12 × 12 feet. Polish people. Property owned by mill. Rent $4.50/mo." [Ca. 1911]   SOURCE: Hine/ LC LC-USZ62-29101.

"Slovenly kitchen-living room of Alfred Benoit, a sweeper in Bennett Mill." Benoit's wife also worked in the mill. New Bedford, Mass., January 1912. SOURCE: Hine/LC LC-USZ62-73985.

Interior of flat of Italian-origin working class family on South Fifth Avenue in New York City, about 1889. SOURCE: Jacob Riis Collection, Library of Congress, Photo No. LC-USZ62-44206.

— 5 —
INCOME AND FAMILY SIZE

The preceding chapter suggests a partial reconciliation of seeming contradictions that appeared in chapters 2 and 3. In chapter 2 we found, as we did not expect, that the total income of Northern foreign-stock families tended to be higher than that of native-stock families including those living in the North. On the basis of this finding we might have expected that Northern foreign-stock families would tend to have better living conditions than Northern and other native-stock groups. In fact, we found in chapter 3 suggestive evidence that the living conditions of the Northern foreign stock may have been worse than those of Northern native-stock families. The living standards of Border State and Southern native-stock families appeared poorer than either of the Northern groups.

We suspected that differences in the size of families accounted for the apparent contradiction between income levels and living standards among Northern foreign- and native-stock families. We found in chapter 2 that native-stock husbands in the North tended to have higher earnings than Northern foreign-stock husbands. However, additional sources of income among the Northern foreign stock, primarily from working children, apparently more than compensated for the lower earnings of foreign-stock husbands. We inferred, therefore, that Northern foreign-stock families probably tended to be larger and to include more older children than the families of the Northern native stock. This inference was confirmed in chapter 4.

Given all this, we probably also inferred that differences in living conditions were related to differences in family size. Larger numbers of children and more older children among the Northern foreign stock may have meant additional income, but that additional income was often not sufficient to compensate for the greater living costs of larger families. The living conditions of the Northern foreign-stock families tended, therefore, to be poorer, despite greater total income, than the conditions of the Northern native stock.

Variations in living standards were not a simple function of variations in income. Differences in family size were also relevant. The task of this chapter is to examine more directly the impact of differences in both family size and income upon living conditions. The goals are to gain a better view of family living conditions and of the factors that affected them.

FAMILY SIZE

Our first step is to directly examine the relationship between family size, income, and living conditions. It will be recalled that we inferred the nature of this relationship indirectly on the basis of the tendency of the Northern foreign stock to have larger families, more working children, older husbands, higher total family income, and poorer living conditions than the native stock. The relation between family size, on the one hand, and income and living conditions, on the other, was not examined directly.

We can carry out this task by cross-tabulating the number of children in families against family income and the percentage of family income spent on food used as an indicator of family living conditions. But before turning to table 5.1 which gives the cross tabulation, we must consider a possible source of distortion: the 729 families that reported income from boarders.

Boarders constituted for these families both a source of income and a burden on income. We might assume that the income provided by boarders exceeded their costs to the families. However, we cannot distinguish those family expenditures and other resources, such as space in dwellings or food, that were used by boarders from those that were used by the families. The consequence is possible distortion of our assessment of the living conditions of these families. To avoid distortion, therefore, families with income from boarders are excluded from table 5.1 and subsequent tables in this chapter. Families that reported the presence of "boarders and others" but reported no income from boarders are included.

For table 5.1, the same income quartiles are employed as in earlier tables, and the quartile distribution of percentage of income spent on food is the same as that used in table 3.5. To simplify the table families are grouped as those with one or no children, those with two or three children, and so on.

As we see, there is some relation between the number of children in families, and family income and the percentage spent on food. In general, the greater the number of children, the higher total family income tended to be. More larger families rank in the highest income quartile than smaller families, while more smaller than larger families rank in the lowest income quartile. Much the same relationship appears in the second panel of table 5.1. Families with larger numbers of children tended to spend a higher

Table 5.1
Number of Children in Families in Relation to
Total Family Income and Percentage of Income Spent on Food*

Table 5.1A: Number of Children in Families and Quartile Distribution of Family Income*

Percentage of Families Within Income Quartile That Have:

Total Family Income Quartile	0-1 Children	2-3 Children	4-5 Children	6 or more Children		Total Number of Families
Fourth Quartile ($741.31-$2,064)	12.9%	28.3%	28.1%	30.7%	100.0%	580
Third Quartile ($558.21-$741.30)	27.2	36.5	22.1	14.2	100.0%	578
Second Quartile ($440.61-$558.20)	35.0	38.7	20.8	5.5	100.0%	583
First Quartile ($110.00-$440.60)	39.3	41.2	14.8	4.7	100.0%	573
						2314

Table 5.1B: Number of Children in Families and Quartile Distribution of Percentage of Income Spent on Food*

Percentage Families With:

Total Family Income Quartile	0-1 Children	2-3 Children	4-5 Children	6 or more Children		Total Number of Families
Fourth Quartile (50.79-149.36%)	17.0%	31.2%	28.5%	23.3%	100.0%	541
Third Quartile (43.56-50.77%)	22.4	38.8	23.6	15.2	100.0%	541
Second Quartile (36.32-43.54%)	30.6	38.8	19.2	11.4	100.0%	595
First Quartile (8.59-36.29%)	41.8	36.1	15.4	6.8	100.0%	637
						2314

*These tables do not include families receiving income from paying boarders.

percentage of income on food than families with smaller numbers of children; the greater the number of children, the higher the percentage of income spent on food. Treating the percentage of income spent on food as an indicator of living conditions, larger families tended to live less well than smaller families. Larger families, in other words, tended to have both higher incomes and poorer living conditions than smaller families.

While table 5.1 indicates some relationship between family size and income and living conditions, it is difficult to assess the strength of those relationships on the basis of the table alone. We can assess the strength of the relationship between two variables, as family size and income in the first panel of the table, by employing measures of association. Such measures yield single numbers (coefficients of association) which reflect the degree of association between the variables of concern. For present purposes we will use a simple measure of association called (for reasons known only to statisticians) *Tau C*.

The calculation of *Tau C* need not concern us. Interpretation of the coefficient is straightforward. It ranges from $+1$ through 0 to -1, with $+1$ indicating perfect positive association, 0 indicating absence of association, and -1 indicating perfect negative association. (In the case of positive associations, the " $+$ " sign is conventionally omitted.) Rounded to two digits, the *Tau C* coefficient for the first panel of table 5.1 is .27 and that for the second panel is .24. Both indicate positive but relatively weak associations.

We can better understand the characteristics of the measure and its interpretation by considering the hypothetical distributions of family size in relation to family income in table 5.2 and comparing those distributions with the actual distributions in table 5.1. Panel A in table 5.2 exemplifies perfect positive association (*Tau C* $= 1.00$) between the number of children in families and income. In this hypothetical distribution, all families fall on the ascending diagonal of cells from the lower left-hand corner of the panel to the upper right-hand corner. As we can see, 100 percent of the first and smallest group of families rank in the lowest income quartile, 100 percent of the next smallest families rank in the second and next to lowest income quartile, 100 percent of the next-to-largest families rank in the third income quartile, and 100 percent of the largest families rank in the highest family income quartile. No deviations from this pattern occur.

The hypothetical distribution in panel B reflects complete absence of association (*Tau C* $= 0.00$) between the number of children in families and family income. All cell entries in the panel are equal. Twenty-five percent of the smallest families rank in the first and lowest income quartile, and so on. The other three categories of family size follow the same pattern. Family size and family income are completely unrelated.

The third hypothetical panel exemplifies perfect negative (or inverse) association at −1.00. The relationship reflected in the panel might be phrased as "the larger the family, the lower the income." All cases fall on the descending diagonal of cells from the upper left-hand corner of the panel to the lower right-hand corner. The pattern is directly opposite that of panel A.

The actual distributions of family size in relation to income and percentage of income spent on food in table 5.1 (*Tau C* = .27) falls between the

Table 5.2
Hypothetical Distribution of Total Number of Children
in Families in Against Quartile Grouping of Total Family Income

Table 5.2A: (Percent Positive Relationship)

	Percentage of Families Within Income Quartile That Have:				
Total Family Income Quartile	0-1 Children	2-3 Children	4-5 Children	6 or more Children	
Fourth Quartile	0.0%	0.0%	0.0%	100.0%	100%
Third Quartile	0.0	0.0	100.0	0.0	100%
Second Quartile	0.0	100.0	0.0	0.0	100%
First Quartile	100.0	0.0	0.0	0.0	100%

Table 5.2B: (Absence of Relationship)

	Percentage of Families Within Income Quartile That Have:				
Total Family Income Quartile	0-1 Children	2-3 Children	4-5 Children	6 or more Children	
Fourth Quartile	25.0%	25.0%	25.0%	25.0%	100.0%
Third Quartile	25.0	25.0	25.0	25.0	100.0
Second Quartile	25.0	25.0	25.0	25.0	100.0
First Quartile	25.0	25.0	25.0	25.0	100.0

Table 5.2C: (Perfect Negative Relationship)

	Percentage of Families Within Income Quartile That Have:				
Total Family Income Quartile	0-1 Children	2-3 Children	4-5 Children	6 or more Children	
Fourth Quartile	100.0%	0.0%	0.0%	0.0%	100.0%
Third Quartile	0.0	100.0	0.0	0.0	100.0
Second Quartile	0.0	0.0	100.0	0.0	100.0
First Quartile	0.0	0.0	0.0	100.0	100.0

distributions in panels A and B of table 5.2. Thus it appears that our expectations with respect to the relationship between these family characteristics are supported, but at relatively low levels. The implication is that other factors in addition to variations in the number of children in families worked to produce variations in family income and living conditions.

MEASURING STANDARDS OF LIVING

With this somewhat modest confirmation of the relationship between the number of children in families and family income and living conditions, we can pursue examination of the relationship between income and family standards of living somewhat farther. In doing so, issues that we touched upon in chapter 3 must be addressed directly. Our central problem is that we have no direct measure of standard of living. In fact, a concept like standard of living cannot be measured directly. Standard of living is an abstract, or "theoretical," concept but only empirical data are available. The best we can do is define standard of living in terms of some empirical indicator. The indicator, however, will never be more than an approximate and imperfect measure of living standards.

Several possible indicators of family living standards have been suggested, including the financial position of families at the end of the year and the percentages of income spent on food, other necessities, and for discretionary purposes. We must keep in mind that these and other indicators of living standards are imperfect and that each touches upon a somewhat different aspect of family life. For present purposes, the percentage of family income spent on food will again be employed.

It is also desirable to employ a second indicator of living conditions and, preferably, one that reflects a different aspect of family life. For this purpose, housing seems a likely candidate. We would probably be willing to assume that, then as now, people tended to prefer more commodious, comfortable, and higher quality housing. If they were able to enjoy better housing we might also assume that their living conditions were better in other ways as well.

Unfortunately, the data collection gives only the number of rooms in family dwellings that were rented. No information is provided about numbers of rooms for the approximately ten percent of the families that owned their houses or for the small number of families (eight) that reported free rent. Similarly, the collection provides no indication of the size of rooms, the quality and nature of construction, the nature of plumbing and sanitation facilities, neighborhood characteristics, or whether the families lived, for example, in tenements, detached houses, or row-houses.

Even so, one measure of the quality of housing conditions and, hence, of living standards is the degree of crowding in dwelling places. We would probably associate greater crowding with poorer living conditions and vice versa. Since the families varied in size, we cannot simply compare income groups in terms of the average or median number of rooms in dwellings. We must employ instead a measure that takes into account both the number of rooms in dwellings and the number of family members. One means is to divide the number of family members by the number of rooms in dwellings. The result is, of course, the number of family members per room.

At least initially we may find fractional numbers of family members per room odd and not entirely meaningful. We can recognize, however, that a value of 1 indicates one person per room regardless of the size of specific dwellings or the number of persons in specific families. A value less than 1 indicates fewer than one family member per room and a value greater than 1 indicates more than one person per room. Thus a value of .5 indicates one person for every two rooms and might reflect a family of two living in four rooms (two family members divided by four rooms) or a family of three in six rooms. Conversely, a family of ten living in five rooms would yield a value of 2 indicating two persons per room, and a family of six living in four rooms (or three living in two rooms) would yield a value of 1.5.

This measure of crowding gains greater intuitive meaning if we recall the activities that families typically carry on in homes—in other words, the activities and relationships that constitute family life. These activities include cooking and preparing food, eating, sleeping, procreating, and the talking, teaching, learning, resting, and recreation that family life involves. And, of course, the names conventionally given to rooms in homes—kitchen, dining room, bedroom, living room, and even family and recreation room —in the present day convey a sense of the diverse elements of family life that are carried on in homes.

With these activities and relationships in mind, we gain an improved notion of the impact of crowding on family life. A family that lives in a single room must, of course, carry on all of these activities in the same room. With a family of four living in two rooms, several of these activities must be carried on in the same room, and it is likely that children and adults sleep in the same room. Even a family that lives in a dwelling with one room per person must carry on some of these activities in the same room.

We can gain an indication of family housing conditions by considering the distribution of families in relation to the number of persons per room in dwellings. This distribution can be calculated for 1,982 of the families. As table 5.3 (p. 104) indicates, of these families approximately sixty (58.3) percent lived in dwellings with one person per room or fewer. Some forty percent of the families lived in more crowded conditions with more than one person per room.

INCOME, FAMILY SIZE, AND LIVING CONDITIONS

Using these indicators of living conditions we can continue our examination of the relationship between family income and living conditions. We need, however, a different approach to measuring income. For some purposes it is useful to measure income in terms of gross amounts received; for others it is not. To use gross amounts in the present case has the effect of treating the families as if they were "all the same"—with the same needs and the same demands upon income. Obviously, families vary in terms of demands upon income if only because they vary in size. Families with larger numbers of members surely cost more to maintain than families with fewer members. We must, therefore, consider income and family size simultaneously.

A simple means by which to do so is to calculate per capita income by dividing total family income by the number of members in families. The resulting measure (or index) standardizes income in relation to family size and indicates the amount of income available to families, regardless of differences in family size or in total income, to support the needs and aspirations of each family member.

The first panel of table 5.4 cross-tabulates the quartile distribution of per capita income against the quartile distribution of the percentage of family income spent on food. The quartile ranges for per capita income are given in the row labels and the ranges for expenditures for necessities in the column headings. The upper boundary of the fourth quartile indicates that

Table 5.3
Density in Dwellings:
Percentage and Number of Families with
Indicated Numbers of Persons Per Room in Dwellings

Persons Per Room in Dwellings	Percentage of Families	Number of Families
0.20 - 0.64	19.3	382
0.65 - 0.99	22.6	448
1.0	16.4	325
1.01-1.51	20.8	413
1.52-5.00	20.9	414
TOTAL	100.0	1,982

Families with income from boarders are excluded.

at least one family is recorded as having spent 149 percent of income on food. In fact, several families reported spending more than 100 percent of income on food and approximately nine percent of the families (224) reported spending more than 100 percent of their income on necessities. Once again we see evidence of end-of-year deficits. Clearly for a significant number of families income was not sufficient, sometimes by a wide margin, to provide food, housing, clothing, and other necessities.

The second panel cross-tabulates the same quartile distributions of per capita income against the families grouped in terms of number of persons per room in dwellings. For this measure, we cannot group the families in quartiles of equal size because of the large number of families with one person per room in dwellings (see table 5.3). Instead, the families are grouped in five categories with the ranges given in the column headings. Families with income from boarders are again excluded from the tabulations.

The relations in table 5.4 are as we expected. The percentage of income spent on food is inversely related to per capita income at a moderate to strong level ($Tau\ C = -.49$). The relationship between per capita income and the measure of family crowding is also negative but somewhat stronger ($Tau\ C = -.56$). In other words, and as we expected, the higher the per capita income, the lower the percentage of family income spent on food and the lower the density in family dwellings.

These associations, moreover, are stronger than those between total family income and the two indicators of family living conditions taken separately. Family income is inversely associated with the percentage of income spent on food ($Tau\ C = -.39$) and unrelated ($Tau\ C = .01$) to the number of persons per room in dwellings. One way to think of the difference between the two income measures is to note that we would be better able to predict the percentage of income families spent on food and the degree of crowding in dwellings if we knew the per capita income of families than if we knew their gross income. Another way is to say that per capita income provides a better explanation of family living conditions than gross income. Still a further way to state the matter is that family living conditions were affected by both family income and family size. The per capita measure takes both income and family size into account and hence explains family living conditions better than either income or family size taken separately.

On the basis of our examination we might be willing to infer that because their families tended to be larger the living conditions of the Northern foreign stock tended to be poorer than those of the Northern native stock. The moderate to strong negative association between the number of children in families, grouped as in table 5.1, and the quartile distribution of per capita income ($Tau\ C = -.47$) further suggests such an inference.

We can also recognize that the relationships in table 5.4 and the coefficients that summarize them are not perfect. They resemble but also diverge significantly from the hypothetical relationship displayed in panel C of table 5.2. In fact, we would surely not expect perfect association between per

Table 5.4

Relationship Between Per Capita Family Income and Two Measures of "Standard of Living" (Spending for Food and Degree of Crowding in Homes)*

Table 5.4A Per Capita Family Income by Quartile Grouping of Percentage of Total Income Spent for Food

Percentage of Families Within Income Quartile Whose
Percent of Total Income Spent on Food Was In:

Per Capita Family Income Quartile	First Quartile (8.6%-36.2)	Second Quartile (36.3%-43.5)	Third Quartile (43.6%-50.7)	Fourth Quartile (50.8%-149)		Total Number of Families
Fourth Quartile ($169.72-$750)	61.7%	23.8%	10.0%	4.4%	99.9%	588
Third Quartile ($124-$169.50)	31.8	33.7	21.5	13.1	100.1%	573
Second Quartile ($89.14-$123.79)	12.8	29.4	33.0	24.8	100.0%	585
First Quartile ($15.71-$89.08)	3.0	15.8	29.2	51.9	99.9	568

Table 5.4B Per Capita Family Income by Quintile Grouping of Number of Persons Per Room in Dwellings

Percentage of Families Within Income Quartile Whose
Number of Persons per Room Was In:

Per Capita Family Income Quartile	First Quintile (.20-.64 Per/Rm.)	Second Quintile (.65-.99 Per/Rm)	Third Quintile (1.0 Per/Rm)	Fourth Quintile (1.01-1.5 Per/Rm)	Fifth Quintile (1.52-5.0 Per/Rm)		Total Number of Families
Fourth Quartile ($170-$750)	54.6%	23.4%	12.0%	8.4%	1.5%	100.0%	474
Third Quartile ($123-$169.73)	19.9	34.2	20.1	17.5	8.3	100.0%	503
Second Quartile ($90.05-$122.88)	4.1	25.6	21.7	28.0	20.6	100.0%	515
First Quartile ($15.71-$90.00)	0.4	6.7	11.2	28.8	52.9	100.0%	490

*These tables do not include families receiving income from boarders.

capita income and the percentage of income spent for necessities or the degree of crowding in family dwellings. Obviously the families differed in other ways than size and income levels. Spending habits undoubtedly differed from family to family, as did needs and preferences; and some families were probably more provident than others. Other factors also intervened. In some areas, for example, because of housing shortages, more commodious housing may have been virtually unavailable whatever the level of family income.

AN ALTERNATIVE APPROACH

The examination above suggests additional relationships between the size of families, income, and living conditions. While it is desirable both to explore these relationships and to take into account additional factors that may have affected them, it would be cumbersome to do so by relying only on the tabular approaches employed to this point. It is also possible that the departures from perfect association seen in the preceding tables and reflected in the coefficients of association are the products in lesser or greater degree of the manner in which we have treated the data. Conversely, it is possible that these approaches work to indicate erroneously high levels of association. To test for these possibilities and to explore additional relationships, we must briefly examine and employ an alternative tool.

In the preceding tables, families are grouped in quartiles in terms of the several income and standard of living measures. While this is a useful procedure for some purposes (for one thing, it provides relatively concrete and understandable descriptive information) it has its limitations and potential liabilities. Within each quartile all families are treated as if they had the same characteristics. To take gross family income as an example, all families in the first quartile are treated as if they had the same level of income, all families in the second quartile as if they also had the same but a higher level of income, and so on.

We know, however, that each family had a specific level of income which varied from one family to another. Grouping the families in quartiles has two adverse consequences. The actual variation (or *variance*) is greatly reduced and capacity to use variance for purposes of analysis and explanation is reduced as well. Grouping also opens the possibility of fallacious inferences. It is possible, for example, that the association between family income and the proportion of income spent on necessities within the quartile groups was different from the association across the four quartile groups. The approach employed in table 5.4 and elsewhere would not detect such differences. It will be clear as well that grouping the families in terms of number of children, as in table 5.1, may have similar consequences.

For some purposes, a better approach is to calculate the association between variables taking all variation in values into account. A commonly used means to do so is by calculating the *product moment correlation* ("Pearson's r") between the variables. Here again, the method of calculating the correlation coefficient (referred to as r) need not be of concern at this point. The coefficient provides an indication of the degree to which two variables are related to each other (or "co-vary") and can be interpreted in somewhat the same fashion as the coefficient of association used above. The correlation coefficient also ranges from 1, indicating perfect positive correlation, through 0, indicating no correlation between the variables, to −1, indicating perfect negative, or inverse, correlation.

Put differently, a negative correlation coefficient between family income and percentage of income spent on necessities would indicate that among the families higher levels of income tended to be related to lower proportions of income spent on necessities. At each higher level of family income, the percentage of income spent on necessities tended to be lower. A positive coefficient would indicate the opposite relationship: as family income increased the percentage of income spent on necessities tended to be higher. (A still different and somewhat more technical way to describe the coefficient is to say that correlation coefficients measure the degree to which the variance characteristic of one variable statistically explains the variance characteristic of a second variable.)

The interpretation of the coefficient can be better understood if we consider the "scatterplot" in figure 5.1. The scatterplot represents the yearly income and the percentage of income spent on necessities for ten hypothetical families. The families range in income from $100 to $950 and the percentage of income which they spent on necessities from a high of 80 percent to a low of 20 percent. Family income is plotted on the horizontal or X axis in the diagram and the percentage of family income spent on necessities on the vertical or Y axis. Each of the dots in figure 5.1 represents the income and percentage of income spent on necessities for one of the families. As can be seen, the lowest-income family had an annual income of $100 and spent 80 percent of income on necessities. The next lowest income family had an income of $110 and spent 68 percent of income on necessities. At the opposite extreme, the highest-income family received $920 and spent 25 percent of income on necessities, and the other seven families range between these extremes.

It should be noted that the variable which is thought to "explain" another variable is conventionally plotted on the horizontal axis and is referred to as the "independent" variable, or X. The variable to be explained is conventionally plotted on the vertical axis and is referred to as the "dependent" variable, or Y.

Figure 5.1 indicates that in the case of these hypothetical families, yearly income and spending for necessities were related. From the distribution of the dots it appears that the higher the income level the lower the percentage spent on necessities and the correlation between the two variables for the ten families is − .91. This relationship can be further clarified by drawing a straight line across the figure that most closely approximates the dots. Through rather cumbersome calculations the unique straight line, called the regression line, can be plotted that "best fits" the scatter of dots by minimizing the distance of the dots from the line. It should be noted that it is the squared distance of the dots from the line that is minimized with the consequence that extreme, or "outlying," cases have a disproportionate effect on the correlation coefficient.

With figure 5.1 in mind it is possible to describe and interpret the correlation coefficient in a different but still nontechnical way. The coefficient can be seen as a measure of the degree to which the cases under consideration—in the present instance, the ten hypothetical families—deviate from the regression line in terms of their values for the two variables. It should be clear that if the dots in the figure had all fallen exactly on the regression line, the correlation coefficient would be 1. To the degree

Figure 5.1
Income And Percentage Of Income Spent On
Necessities For Ten Hypothetical Families

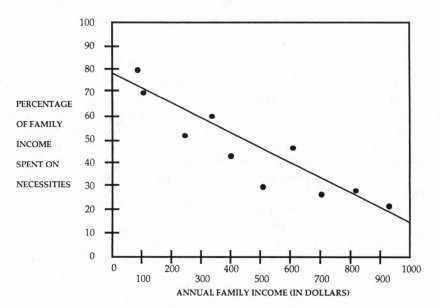

that the dots do not fall exactly on the line, the coefficient falls to fractional values. It should also be clear that if the scatter of the dots and the regression line had extended from the lower left-hand segment of the figure to the upper right-hand segment, the coefficient would have been positive; if the dots had fallen exactly on such a line the value of the coefficient would have been 1. (Again, when the coefficient is positive the plus sign is conventionally omitted.)

This procedure also produces a second statistic, called the *regression coefficient*, which will be employed in subsequent chapters and can conveniently be considered at this point. The regression coefficient (referred to as b or sometimes as the "slope coefficient" or simply the "slope") summarizes the amount of difference in the dependent variable (Y) associated with a difference of one unit in the independent variable (X). For the distribution in figure 5.1, b = −.064. In other words, in the case of the distribution in figure 5.1, an increase of one dollar in income was associated with a decrease of −.064 percentage points in the percentage of income spent on necessities.

It will be recognized that the relationship depicted in figure 5.1 can be also be described in terms of the familiar equation for a straight line:

$$Y = a + bX$$

where a is the intercept and defined as the value of Y when the value of X is zero and b is the amount of difference in Y associated with one unit of difference in X. Using figure 5.1, the value of the intercept (a) is 77.47 and the value of the regression coefficient (b) is -.064. Thus the equation becomes:

$$Y = 77.47 - .064X$$

Any value of X is associated with an expected value of Y which can be calculated using the values of the intercept (a) and the regression coefficient (b). Returning to the distribution in figure 5.1, an increase of one dollar in income was associated with an expected .064 decrease in the percentage of income spent on necessities. A family with an income of $600 would have an expected percentage of income spent on necessities of 39.07. In other words, the family's income times the regression coefficient ($600 × .064 = 38.40) minus the intercept term (77.47) equals the expected percentage (39.07) of income spent in necessities. Similarly, a family with an income of $400 would have an expected percentage of income spent on necessities of 51.87 (77.47 − .064 × $400). It will be clear that if the relation in figure 5.1 had been positive, with the regression line sloping upward, the equation would be

$$Y = a + bX$$

and the value of (bX) would be added to a to calculate the expected value of Y in any given case.[1]

Keeping the preceding discussion and figure 5.1 in mind, we can employ the correlation procedure to continue our examination of the relationships between family size, income, and living standards. Our first step is to reexamine the relationships between the several variables considered earlier in this chapter in order to discover whether categorizing families in quartiles or other groups may have had misleading consequences. The second step is to examine the direct relationship between family size and the indicators of living standards and between gross and per capita income.

The *correlation matrix* in table 5.5 gives the correlation coefficient for each pair of variables indicated at the head of each column and at the beginning of each row. Thus the correlation between the number of children in families and total family income is .44, the correlation between total family income and the percentage of income spent on food is −.34, and so on.

We can note that the correlation coefficients in the table are somewhat

Table 5.5
Product-Moment Correlations Between Selected Variables Measuring Family Income, Family Size, and "Standard of Living"*

	Per Capita Family Income	Total Family Income	Percent of Total Income Spent on Food	Number of Persons per Room in Dwellings	Total Number of Children in Family
Per Capita Total Family Income	1.00				
Total Family Income	.39	1.00			
Percent of Total Income Spent on Food	-.55	-.34	1.00		
Number of Persons per Room in Dwelling	-.57	.01	.28	1.00	
Total Number of Children in Family	-.53	.44	.28	.62	1.00

* Families with income from boarders are excluded.

higher than the comparable coefficients of association given in preceding sections. As an example, the coefficient of association (*Tau C*) between the number of children in families and gross family income is .27 while the correlation coefficient (r) is .44. Similarly the relationship between per capita income and the number of persons per room in homes appears only slightly stronger in table 5.5 (r = −.57) than in the preceding section (*Tau C* = −.53). Total family income again appears unrelated to the number of persons per room in dwellings. It may be, then, that grouping the data in the preceding sections tended to reduce the apparent relationship between variables. However, the differences between the correlation coefficients and the coefficients of association are relatively small and the signs are the same. The correlations coefficients, therefore, do not challenge generalizations in the preceding sections.

The correlations between the number of children in families, per capita income, and the two measures of family living conditions are also as we expected. The number of children in families is positively related to total family income (r = .44), negatively related to per capita income at a moderate to strong level (r = −.53), positively related to the percentage of income spent on food but at a relatively low level (r = .28), and positively related at a moderate to strong level (r = .62) to the number of family members per room in dwellings. (In other words, the larger the families the greater the crowding in homes.) It appears, in short, that larger families contributed not only to higher total family income but also to lower per capita income, a greater percentage of income spent on food, and greater crowding in homes. Put still differently, in terms of the measures used here larger families tended to contribute to poorer living conditions.

The relationships between total and per capita income and the measures of living standards are somewhat more surprising. Total family income is related to per capita family income (r = .39). As we expected, the higher the total income, the higher the per capita income, but as we also expected the relationship is less than perfect. Total income and per capita income, in keeping with prior expectations, are negatively related to the percentage of income spent on food. The relationship, however, is somewhat stronger in the case of the per capita income measure (r = −.55) than in the case of total income (r = −.34). In contrast, total income is effectively unrelated to the crowding measure (r = .01) while per capita income is negatively related at a moderate to strong level (r = −.57) to the crowding measure.

GENERALIZATIONS AND QUALIFICATIONS

This chapter is concerned with the relationship between family income and the size of families, on the one hand, and family living conditions, on the other. The argument is that differences in family living conditions were produced by the interaction of family income and family size. Larger families sometimes had more working members and higher total family income than smaller families with fewer working members, as we would expect. On the other hand, larger families also meant more mouths to feed and more bodies to house and clothe, and the greater earnings of larger families were often not sufficient to compensate for these added burdens. The further argument would be that larger families were often a disadvantage in economic terms.

At first glance the argument may seem virtually self-evident, and we might ask why so much is made of so little. Further thought leads us, however, to questions and reservations. One set of questions involves the manner in which family income and family size are combined to assess their joint effects on living conditions. The manner in which family living conditions are measured should also give rise to questions in terms of the adequacy of the two indicators. Still a third set of questions and reservations concerns the possibility that other factors in addition to income and family size affected family living conditions.

We can also ask, as well, what the chapter tells us about actual family living conditions and about differences in living conditions from one group of families to the other. It is easy enough to compare the several regional and nationality groups in terms of the indicators employed above. When we do so we gain a more concrete view of family living conditions. For these purposes table 5.6 gives the median per capita income, percentage of income spent on food, and number of persons per room in dwellings for

Table 5.6:
Selected Indicators of Family Living Conditions
by Regional and Nationality Groups

	Median Per Capita Income	Median Percent of Income Spent on Food	Median Percent of Income Surplus of Deficit	Median Numbers of Persons per Room
Native-Stock Families in the North	$ 137.60	38.8%	5.9%	.74
Foriegn-Stock Families in the North	128.80	44.0	1.1	.96
Native-Stock Families in Border States	112.00	43.7	2.0	1.20
Native-Stock Families in the South	95.00	41.8	0	1.61

native- and foreign-stock families residing in the North and for native-stock families in the Southern and Border States. To provide an improved basis for comparison a fourth indicator of living conditions is added—the median end-of-year financial positions of the family calculated as a percentage of family income.

The table is about as we would expect given what we know of the income levels and family size of the four groups. In terms of all four indicators of living conditions the Northern native-stock families appear consistently better off than the other groups. These families had higher per capita incomes and a higher percentage of surplus income, spent a smaller percentage of income on food, and were less crowded in dwellings.

In general terms, table 5.6 supports generalizations to the effect that larger families tended to be a disadvantage in economic terms and that the tendency of some groups to have larger numbers of children and, perhaps, to encourage children to remain at home until an older age often contributed to poorer living conditions. These generalizations immediately give rise to questions of another sort. Some of these concern the reasons for variations in the number of children which may, in turn, raise questions about some of our indicators of living conditions. We have suggested that larger numbers of children and encouraging children to remain at home until an older age may have been a more-or-less conscious strategy to maximize family income and living conditions. If so, this chapter suggests, the strategy was often unsuccessful.

We can think, however, of noneconomic reasons for larger families and for encouraging children to remain at home. These surely include religious tenets, the inadequacy of available approaches to contraception, and simple preferences for more rather than fewer children. That some people may simply have preferred more to fewer children raises a question concerning the validity of some of the indicators of living conditions employed in this chapter. Larger families are sometimes seen as providing greater interdependence, closer interaction and cohesion, and a warmer life experience than smaller ones. Is it possible that conditions that seem to us seriously crowded were actually seen by some people of the time as beneficial and desirable?

TO THE READER

We return in this section to the measures and indicators employed in the preceding pages. One goal is to assess the strengths and limitations of these measures and indicators. A second is to consider factors in addition to those of income and family size that may have affected family living conditions.

By so doing we can gain a better view of the living conditions of more specific regional and nationality groups.

It will be apparent that examination of the families in terms of per capita income rather than total family income involves a significant shift in perspective. By examining the levels and sources of total family income we gain an indication of the ways in which the families gained their livelihoods and of the degree to which they shared in the benefits of national productivity. The level of total income also provides a limited indication of family living conditions. By taking differences in family size into account, per capita income gives us an indication of the amounts available to support each family member. Another way to put it is to say that the per capita income measure holds family size constant and allows us to meaningfully compare families of different sizes.

We can see the significance and implication of this shift in perspective by reconsidering the income levels of the three families described in chapter 1. The family described in the letter reproduced in that chapter had an annual income of $576, Family 121 an income of $1043, and Family 82 an income of $525 for the year. Viewed in these terms, the income of the family described in the letter amounted to approximately 55 percent of that of Family 121 and the income of Family 82 roughly 50 percent of that of Family 121. From this perspective the income of Family 82 appears only modestly below that of the family described in the letter, and the income of both families appears well below that of Family 121.

Using per capita income, the comparisons are quite different. With seven members (or should it be six?), the per capita income of the family described in the letter was approximately $82 for the year; the per capita income for the nine members of Family 82 was roughly $58; and that of the five members of Family 121 was approximately $209. In terms of per capita income, the income of the family described in the letter was roughly 40 percent of that of Family 121; the per capita income of Family 82 some 28 percent of the income of Family 121 and 71 percent of that of the family in the letter. Clearly, the income disparities between the families appear different depending upon whether per capita income or total family income is considered.

(As a further question, however, what is the justification for treating all family members as the same regardless of age or other differences? Do family members of different ages consistently impose the same burdens on income? Is an alternative approach available?)

We can recognize that, like the measure of per capita income, the several measures of family living conditions employed in this chapter and elsewhere in this volume all have limitations. Each of the measures relates to a particular aspect of family life, and we would not necessarily expect families to differ in precisely the same ways in all aspects of life. We can also recognize that other factors in addition to income and family size undoubtedly affected family living conditions. We might phrase the questions as follows: In what ways did the families differ from one aspect of life to another, and what other factors affected family living conditions apart from income and family size?

One way to evaluate the measures and to address these questions is to return to the relationship between per capita income and the indicators of living conditions and ask how well per capita income predicts (or explains) differences in the several indicators. If we assumed (1) that the several measures are completely valid and exactly measure what we claim for them, (2) that the families differed from each other in the same way in all aspects of life, and (3) that income and family size were the only factors that effected family living conditions we would expect a particular pattern of correlations between the measures. More specifically we would expect per capita income to be correlated with the percentage of family income spent on food at the level of − 1.0, with the end-of-year surpluses or deficits at 1.0, and with the number of persons per room in dwellings at − 1.0.

We know, however, that none of these assumptions are completely valid, and that the actual correlations (the product moment correlations discussed above) are quite different. Per capita income is correlated with the percentage of family income spent on food at the level of − .55, with end-of-year surpluses and deficits at .49, and with the number of persons per room in dwellings at − .57, all well below the levels indicated above.

On the other hand, these are moderately strong correlations. They suggest that per capita income does provide a useful mean to predict (explain) differences between the families as measured by the several indicators of living conditions. In other words, the correlations are compatible with the view that some of the variations in living conditions among the families were the result of differences in per capita income—or, more accurately, of differences in family income and family size. The actual correlations depart from unity and the degree of departure suggests the degree to which the three assumptions sketched above are invalid.

We could go a step further and find indications of the specific ways in which the assumptions are invalid. For this purpose table 5.7 gives the median values for these same indicators for each of the eight regional and nationality groups examined in earlier sections. The first thought might be that the several groups ought to rank in terms of median values in approximately the same order as they rank in terms of per capita income. To better compare rankings, the families are ordered in the table in terms of their ranking on per capita income.

As we see, there are many deviations from this ranking. The British and native-stock families rank highest in per capita income. They also appear relatively better off in terms of the indicators of living conditions, although the pattern is more consistent for the native stock than for the British. On the other hand, the Southern native-stock families and the two groups of Canadians in the North rank at the bottom in per capita income and also appear least well off, although exceptions can be noted. In general, however, the ordering of groups in terms of per capita income no more than approximates their ordering in relation to the measures of living conditions. When we ask why the orderings fall short of correspondence, several reasons are obvious and with further thought additional possibilities come to mind.

One reason is statistical. The correlations between per capita income and the several indicators of living conditions are imperfect, hence at best no more than approximate correspondence between the rankings can be expected. In any event, the correlation across the entire group of families taking each family individually would not necessarily be the same as the ranking of groups of families. At best, the correlation across the entire set of families suggests expectations about the ranking of groups.

Other reasons are less technical. One concerns the approach to calculating per capita income that was referred to above. Would we really expect that young children, as examples, would impose the same burdens on family income as older children? Is it the case that the discussion to this point has implicitly assumed that prices and the availability of commodities were the

Table 5.7
Selected Indicators of Family Living Conditions
by Place of Residence and Specific Nationality

	Median Per Capita Income	Median Percent of Income Spent on Food	Median Percent of Income Surplus of Deficit	Median Numbers of Persons per Room
Northern British	$141.00	41.7%	2.4%	.85
Northern Native Stock	137.60	38.8	5.9	.74
Northern Irish	132.50	44.2	1.1	.97
Northern Continental European	129.50	41.7	4.7	.94
Border State Native Stock	112.00	43.7	2.0	1.20
Northern French Canadian	106.50	48.0	-1.0	1.27
Northern Canadian	99.00	49.8	-1.8	.99
Southern Native Stock	95.00	41.8	.0	1.61

same in all areas and that the same level of income would support the same standard of living in all areas? Is such an assumption tenable? Is it possible that some groups were able to supplement their income in ways that are not reflected in the indicators?

— 6 —
FAMILY LIVING CONDITIONS:
A SECOND LOOK

The goal of this chapter is to improve our understanding of family circumstances and the factors that affected them. As a first step, we again examine family spending to gain a better view of differences in living conditions at different levels of income. By marshaling limited price information this view is made more concrete, although it remains an approximation.

A further step involves examination of expenditures as percentages of income. We have two reasons for doing so, both suggested at earlier points. We would probably be willing to assume that the lower the percentage of income spent for necessities, the higher the general standard of living. Secondly, we would probably also assume that the choices families made in spending income that remained after meeting the requirements of necessities reflected their values and preferences.

Throughout our examination, the relationship between family living conditions and other family characteristics is considered. In the preceding chapter we found that family living conditions were affected both by the actual level of income and by the number of family members to support. We know that other factors, some of them unmeasurable, were also relevant, including, for example, variations in prices from one area to another, and buying and housekeeping practices. Even so, all other things being the same, small families were able to live better at the same level of income than larger families.

Differences in the size of families raise additional questions. As we know, several categories of families tend to be small. Younger couples often have smaller families because they have had less time to have children. The families of older couples are frequently small because children have left home, and some couples, regardless of age, simply prefer fewer or no children. Undoubtedly, all three of these considerations affected the size of the families of textile workers, but we could usefully think of a kind of family "life cycle" from small in the early years of marriage, to larger in the middle, years, to small, again in the later years.

Following this view we might suspect that in higher income families, with higher living standards and fewer children, parents tended to be older than in lower income families. We might surmise that in many of these families, children had already left home, possessions had been accumulated with the result of smaller needs, and husbands enjoyed higher wages due to greater experience, promotions, and other advancements gained through the years. In fact we might see the higher incomes and better standards of living enjoyed by some families as a reflection of their stage in the family life cycle.

Many of us would find this an appealing notion. It is pleasant to believe that through effort, prudence, and, perhaps, self-denial during the younger years people in these days were able to enjoy a more comfortable and better life in their middle and later years. Certainly, hypotheses are suggested that merit consideration. We will find, however, that a variety of factors in addition to effort and providence shaped the experiences and opportunities of textile workers and their families.

A PROFILE OF THE FAMILIES

Table 6.1 gives us a summary view of family living conditions and other characteristics. The families are grouped in income quartiles, but using per capita income rather than gross family income. (See table 5.4 for the appropriate quartile ranges.) Panel A of the table gives the median amounts spent per person for various purposes. The panel also gives the median end-of-year family surpluses and deficits, again treated on a per capita basis. Panel B of the table gives, also as medians, per capita income, earnings of husbands, and total income. Median number of children and age of husbands are given in panel C, along with the median number of rooms and the median number of persons per room in dwellings.

The expenditure categories used are essentially the same as those used in table 3.1. As in chapter 3 the food and clothing categories summarize all expenditures for these purposes including in the food category unspecified "other food costs." The housing category includes expenditures for rent, fuel, lighting, furniture and utensils, and taxes, assuming that the amounts recorded in the data collection as paid for taxes were property taxes. Spending for sickness and death is self-explanatory. Spending for "discretionary purposes" includes such diverse purposes as life insurance, labor and other organizations, religion and charity, books and newspapers, amusements and vacations, and liquor and tobacco. The "other expenses" category is an unaccounted category which includes all unspecified spending for commod-

Table 6.1
Median Per Capita Expenditures and Family Characteristics
by Quartile Distribution of Per Capita Family Income

Table 6.1A: Per Capita Expenditures

	Families with Per Capita Income in:			
	First Quartile	Second Quartile	Third Quartile	Fourth Quartile
Food	$36.47	$47.47	$57.48	$75.49
Clothing	11.62	16.38	20.65	26.63
Household	15.53	23.44	30.79	43.85
Sickness & Death	1.98	2.09	2.51	2.93
Discretionary	3.26	5.35	8.25	13.12
Other Expenses	2.65	4.16	5.89	8.78
End-of-year Financial Position	-2.92	0.38	9.85	36.99

Table 6.1B: Family Income

	Families with Per Capita Income in:			
	First Quartile	Second Quartile	Third Quartile	Fourth Quartile
Per Capita Income	$ 71.5	$105.4	$144.3	$213.8
Husbands' Earnings	322.5	399.9	441.5	509.3
Total Income	438.3	539.3	619.3	681.4

Table 6.1C: Dwelling and Family Characteristics

	Families with Per Capita Income in:			
	First Quartile	Second Quartile	Third Quartile	Fourth Quartile
Number of Rooms in Dwellings	3.6	4.3	4.6	4.7
Number of Persons per Room	1.6	1.0	0.8	0.6
Number of Children	3.9	2.6	1.7	0.5
Age of Husband	37.8	36.6	36.8	40.7

ities and purposes other than food. In using these classifications, we must recall the caveats noted in chapter 3.

The table gives, as we would expect, an impression of significantly different family circumstances moving from the lowest to the highest income group. Median per capita spending for most purposes—food, housing, clothing, discretionary purposes and sickness and death as well as the unaccounted category—progressively increases across the four income groups, although differences in per capita expenses for sickness and death are small. The end-of-year financial position of the families improves from a median per capita deficit of slightly less than $3 among families in the lowest income quartile to a median per capita surplus of almost $37 among families in the highest quartile.

The second panel of table 6.1 indicates that all three measures of family income systematically increase from the lowest to the highest income quartile. Obviously, per capita income increases but so also does total family income and income from the earnings of husbands. This pattern of income differences is as we expected. We will also recognize, however, that some families with relatively high *per capita* incomes had lower total incomes and lower husbands' earnings than families with lower per capita incomes. In some families low total income or low husbands' earnings were compensated for by fewer family members.

As we see in Panel C, the number of children in families consistently declines from a median of 3.9 among families in the lowest per capita income quartile to a median of .5 in families in the highest quartile. The higher the total family income *and* the smaller the family, the higher the per capita income and, so it appears, the better the family living conditions. As we expected, higher income families also appear less crowded in dwellings reflecting both modestly larger dwellings and smaller numbers of children among these families.

The evidence to this point is compatible with the family life-cycle formulation sketched at the beginning of this chapter. That is, to this point table 6.1 is compatible with the view that as husbands aged they gained experience, skills, and seniority, received promotions and wage increases, or were able to move to better and higher paying employment. At the same time, family size declined as children grew older and left home. With better wages and fewer family members to support, per capita income and family living conditions were better.

Unfortunately, examination of the age of husbands provides little support for the life-cycle formulation. As we see, the median age of husbands tended to increase from the lowest to the highest per capita income quartile, but the differences are inconsistent and small. In median age, husbands in the highest per capita income were only about three years older than those in the lowest quartile and approximately four years older than those in the second and third quartiles. Moreover, the correlation between the age and earnings of husbands is low and negative (r = −.16). In short, table 6.1 does not provide consistent support for the life-cycle formulation.

We will return to this formulation at a later point. The discussion here has treated the families as a group without regard to regional, nationality, or other differences. It is possible that more detailed examination taking such differences into account would provide greater support for that formulation. Alternatively, that examination may suggest that the life cycle notion of family prosperity was mitigated by other factors.

CLOTHING

In the preceding section we gained a better view of family expenditures at different levels of per capita income and an indication of the relationship between family size, income, and living conditions. Our discussion, however, did not provide an indication of the amounts of specific commodities that families were able to, and chose to, purchase or of the adequacy of these purchases in terms of living conditions. We can take a step in this direction by more closely examining family expenditures for clothing— obviously, one of the basic necessities. To do so, we will require a number of assumptions and inferences.

We can begin by examining clothing expenditures for different family members. As table 6.2 indicates, total expenditures for clothing tended to increase across the first three income quartiles. In contrast clothing expenditures among families in the highest income quartile were below those of families in the third quartile and very slightly below families in the second quartile.

Table 6.2
Median Family Clothing Expenditures by Quartile
Distribution of Per Capita Family Income

Families with Per Capita Income in:

	First Quartile	Second Quartile	Third Quartile	Fourth Quartile
Total Clothing Expenditures	$71.5	$79.9	$85.0	$79.6
Husbands' Clothing	15.9	20.0	24.5	29.1
Wives' Clothing	9.8	14.7	19.1	24.2
Childrens' Clothing	39.7	39.8	35.2	17.8

Differences in total clothing expenditures conceal more complex differences between income groups. Expenditures for children's clothing were
approximately the same for families in the first and second income quartiles,
lower among families in the third quartile, and very substantially lower for
the highest per capita income families, as we may have expected. The
differences of course, reflect, the tendency of higher income families to
include smaller numbers of children. In contrast, spending for clothing for
wives and husbands is consistently greater moving from the lowest to the
highest income quartile. We should particularly note the lower spending
for clothing for wives than for husbands among the lowest income families.

In more general terms, the table suggests that with smaller numbers of
children and higher incomes, families were able to spend less for children's
clothing and more for clothing for husbands and wives. Because of fewer
children, husbands and wives in the highest income category were apparently able to dress better while still spending less for clothing.

Table 6.2 suggests differences in clothing expenditures in relation to
income and family size. On the other hand, the table gives us no information as to the specific items of clothing that families could, and did, buy, nor
does it allow us to assess the adequacy of family clothing. We can develop
inferences on both of these counts, but only by confronting two major
obstacles.

In the first place, the data collection gives us only the amounts spent on
clothing; no information is given as to the kinds, number of items, and
quality of clothing actually purchased. Moreover, fully adequate information
bearing upon clothing prices is not available for these years. While we can
estimate prices they give us only a basis for inferring the amounts and
nature of clothing purchased. As will be recognized, even if we had fully
adequate price information we would still be able to estimate only the
amounts, quality, and kinds of clothing that families *could have* purchased
and not the amounts and kinds *actually* purchased.

The second set of obstacles is more complex. To assess the adequacy of
the clothing that families were able to purchase would require some sort of
standard of comparison. One standard that we might think of would be
whether family members considered their clothing inadequate—whether
or not, in other words, they felt deprived. However, people can feel deprived at different levels. Just as would be true today, some textile workers
and their families may have felt deprived even though their clothing was as
good and abundant as that of other families who did not feel deprived. This
is clearly a subjective standard, and we have no information as to whether
any or all of the family members considered themselves deprived because
of inadequate clothing.

We can also conceive of an objective standard of adequacy. Such a standard might be the clothing required to provide necessary warmth, protection from the weather, and to meet the standards of modesty according to the conventions of the time. We can recognize that this would be a minimal standard which few at the time would have considered adequate. In any event, we have no such objective standard.

As a third approach, we might base a standard of adequacy upon the judgments and opinions of the time as to what constituted adequate clothing. This standard would reflect judgments of the time of the adequacy of clothing in terms of both warmth and protection while also giving regard to such considerations as cleanliness, appearance, perhaps matters of style, and the different social, work, and other situations in which people must participate.

As it happens, a number of scholars, government officials, observers, and commentators at the end of the nineteenth century and thereafter invested considerable effort in assessing living conditions and developing standards of adequacy. Extensive price information was also assembled, particularly through a congressional investigation conducted in 1908. A detailed study by William B. Hartley draws on this information to estimate an income "poverty line" for the years from 1870 through 1914. Income below this line is considered insufficient to support an adequate standard of living. The discussion of family clothing standards and expenditure that follows draws upon this study.[1]

Table 6.3, which is adapted from the Hartley study, gives us a means to assess in more concrete ways both the nature and adequacy of the clothing expenditures of the families—if, that is, we make certain assumptions and inferences. The table gives for husbands, wives and male and female children aged ten through thirteen the items of clothing and the number of each estimated as required each year for an adequate standard of living. The costs of these items are also given and sum to an estimated yearly clothing budget required to provide adequate clothing.

The estimates used in the table involve several assumptions, among them that children of ten through thirteen were "representative." The clothing requirements of children over thirteen are presumed to be greater and more costly than those of children ten to thirteen, while the requirements of children under ten would be less costly. The differing requirements of older and younger children would therefore "balance out," so that the requirements of children ten to thirteen allow estimation of the clothing requirements of all children.

When we compare the estimated clothing requirements of husbands and wives given in table 6.3 with actual yearly expenditures given in table 6.2, the result may seem surprising. Only the actual expenditures for clothing for husbands and wives in the highest per capita income quartile meet the minimum standard and then only the lower standard for the South. Expenditures for clothing for husbands and wives in all other income categories fall below the minimum standard.

Our comparisons, of course, are not completely valid. Table 6.3 provides differing standards for the North and the South reflecting differences in prices and the lesser clothing needs of the latter region. However, calculation of actual clothing expenditures by textile workers and their families taking region of residence into account reveals much the same pattern of

Table 6.3
Standards of Family Clothing from William Burton Hartley,
Estimation of the Incidence of Poverty in the United States, 1870 to 1914 (a)
with 1907 Prices for Selected Areas

Husband

Item	Number	Price for Southern Mill Workers	Price for Massachusetts Mill Worker
Suit	1	$8.00	$8.00
Overcoat	1	(NA)	4.00
Trousers	2	2.00	3.00
Light Shirt	1	1.00	1.00
Colored Shirt	4	1.00	1.00
Overalls	3	2.25	1.50
Winter Underwear	2	(NA)	2.00
Summer Underwear	2	2.00	2.00
Shoes	3	7.00	7.00
Stockings	6	.60	.60
Hats	2	1.00	1.00
Collars	4	.50	.50
Necktie	1	.25	.50
Suspenders	1	.25	.25
Handkerchiefs	3	.30	.30
Total Costs		$26.15	$32.65

Wife

Item	Number	Price for Southern Mill Workers	Price for Massachusetts Mill Worker
Suit	1	5.75	(NA)
Coat	1	(NA)	5.00
Waist, wool	1	(NA)	1.60
Skirt, wool	1	(NA)	6.25
Gingham or Calico Dresses	3	2.25	2.85
Petticoats	2	.72	1.20
Drawers	2	.25	.40
Undershirts	2	.50	.70
Hats or Head Coverings	2	2.00	2.00
Stockings (pairs)	6	1.50	2.00
Gingham Aprons	2	.50	(NA)
Shoes (pairs)	2	3.00	3.00
Handkerchiefs	4	.20	.25
Gloves (pair)	1	.50	.50
Calico Waists	3	.72	.54
Calico or Duck Skirts	2	.80	1.80
Total Costs		$18.69	$28.09

differences suggested by comparison of table 6.2 and 6.3. The median actual expenditures for husbands' clothing was $24.20 for the Northern states, $19.50 for the Border states, and $19.40 for the South. The comparable figures for wives are $17.80, $9.90, and $13.50. In each region, in short, the actual expenditures of more than half of the families for clothing for husbands and wives are well below the standards given in table 6.3.

Using a few simple calculations, and several assumptions, rough comparisons can also be made between actual expenditures for children and total family expenditures, on the one hand, and the standards given in table 6.3

Table 6.3: continued

Sons of Ages 10-13

Item	Number	Price for Southern Mill Workers	Price for Massachusetts Mill Worker
Suit	1	$3.50	$4.00
Overcoat	1	(NA)	3.00
Trousers	4	2.00	2.00
Shirts	4	1.20	1.20
Winter Underwear	2	1.00	2.00
Summer Underwear	2	1.00	2.00
Hats	2	.50	.50
Suspenders (pairs)	1	.25	.25
Stockings (pairs)	6	2.00	2.50
Shoes (pairs)	3	4.50	6.00
Total Costs		$15.95	$23.45

Daughters of Ages 10-13

Item	Number	Price for Southern Mill Workers	Price for Massachusetts Mill Worker
Wool Dress	1	(NA)	2.00
Gingham Dress	5	3.10	3.65
Coat	1	(NA)	2.00
Cotton Petticoats	2	.50	.80
Drawers	2	.25	.25
Winter Undershirts	2	.50	.50
Hats	2	2.00	1.00
Stockings	6	1.50	1.50
Mittens (pairs)	1	(NA)	.25
Shoes	3	6.00	7.50
Ribbons		.50	.50
Total Costs		$14.35	$19.95
Total Costs for Family of Four		$75.14	$104.14

(a) Unpublished Doctoral Dissertation, University of Wisconsin, 1969.

(NA) Not ascertained or not applicable.

on the other. If we assume that the number of sons and daughters were approximately equal among the families, then an average minimal clothing budget for children ten to thirteen of both sexes can be estimated (by summing the requirements for boys and girls given by Hartley and dividing by two). We can then multiply these averages by the median number of children in each region to create a new estimate of the costs of providing adequate clothing for children. The further assumptions are that children ten to thirteen were representative of all children as discussed above. By summing these estimates with the estimated requirements for husbands and wives, we can estimate the total expenditures required to provide adequate clothing taking into account variations in the number of children in families. Our recalculated standards of minimal adequacy are given in table 6.4.

By comparing these standards with median actual clothing expenditures in each region (also given in table 6.4), we can assess the adequacy of family clothing. The result is again surprising. In all categories, median family expenditures for clothing are well below the levels estimated as adequate. The magnitude of these differences can be summarized by considering the second panel of the table, which calculates the standards as percentages of actual expenditures and actual expenditures as percentages of the standards. As can be seen, for example, the standard for Southern husbands appears as 133 percent of actual expenditures and actual expenditures as 75 percent of the standard. Taking the table at face value, the conclusion must be that in well over half of the families clothing expenditures were insufficient to provide adequate clothing according to a reasonable standard.

Table 6.4
Re-estimated Hartley Standard and Median Actual Clothing Expenditures by Region

	South and Border		North	
	Re-estimated Standard	Actual Expenditures	Re-estimated Standard	Actual Expenditures
Husband	$26.15	$19.6	$32.65	$24.0
Wife	18.69	13.5	28.09	17.9
Per Child	15.15	12.9	21.70	14.9
	Standard as Percent of Actual Expenditures	Actual Expenditures as Percent of Standard	Standard as Percent of Actual Expenditures	Actual Expenditures as Percent of Standard
Husband	133%	75%	136%	74%
Wife	138	72	157	64
Per Child	117	85	146	69

But is the standard reasonable and are the comparisons sensible? Is it plausible to believe that so many families fell so far below standards of adequate clothing as the comparisons suggest? We can gain some insight into these uncertainties by considering three broad questions.

Our first question concerns the price and cost information we have used. Is it valid to use clothing prices as of 1908 to estimate clothing purchases and standards in 1888 through 1890 (when the data on textile workers and their families were collected?) Fragmentary data on clothing prices for the earlier years are available. Comparison of this information with the more complete information for 1908 indicates that in the earlier years the prices for some items of clothing were probably higher while those of other items were lower, but that the average was probably the same for the two periods. Moreover, the Consumer Price Index for 1888, 1889, and 1890 was 27. The index for 1907 stood at 28. While we cannot infer that clothing prices, and the prices for specific items of clothing, fluctuated in the same way as all other commodities, the suggestion is relative price similarity. Thus our best answer to the question seems to be that clothing prices were probably approximately the same, or if anything slightly lower, in the years 1888 through 1890 than in 1908.

Our second question concerns the clothing standards used in table 6.3. As one issue, the estimates are based on the prices for "coarser" grades of clothing, but it is likely that families sometimes chose to purchase fewer but better clothes. The implications of this possibility for the validity of the standards are unclear.

The larger issue is whether the standards are excessive. Were all of these items really necessary in the amounts indicated? Did a man need a new suit each year, or could he have got along with a new suit every other year? Here we should note that in these years men, even manual laborers, often wore suits to work. The estimate really is that a suit would be worn "for good" for one year and "for work" for a second year. If we think about it, similar questions can be raised in the case of other items.

In considering these questions we should recall the nature of the estimates. People at that time, as people today, went to church, attended social functions, and transacted business, so that matters of appearance were of consequence. Our estimates of minimal clothing standards include appearance and the different situations and occasions in which people participated. They involve, in short, an effort to estimate what was required to maintain a "decent" standard of dress as well as to meet the minimal requirements of warmth, protection, and modesty.

Our third question involves supplementary sources of clothing. Undoubtedly, clothing was sometimes given away to some families; some families probably purchased used clothing; and in some families clothing was surely "handed down" from older to younger children. The larger issue may be that many women in these years sewed and made clothing at home. The point is suggested by the many families that owned sewing machines, judging from the descriptions of the households provided by interviewers. We might also assume that since these were textile workers, some may have bought cloth at reduced prices and in this way further increased the economic advantages of making clothes at home. Unfortunately, at this point we have no way to assess the magnitude and incidence of such supplements to family clothing.

On the other hand, we can take additional steps toward assessing the plausibility of our comparisons. It can be recognized that the comparisons probably err on the conservative side and that family clothing was probably better than the comparisons suggest. Clothing prices may have been lower in the years 1888 through 1890 than those used in making the comparisons; the standards of adequacy employed may be excessive; and many families undoubtedly supplemented their ready-to-wear clothing with home made clothes. On these grounds, we can assume that the families were on the average better off than the comparisons suggest. The comparisons constitute, in short, a "worst case" analysis.

With this worst case characteristic in mind we can make a further assessment of plausibility—one that considers margins of error. If we assume that the discrepancies between median actual expenditures for clothing and estimated standards of adequacy were actually the product of error or of the inadequacy of data, how large must these errors and inadequacies be to account for the discrepancies?

Examination of table 6.4 using the clothing of Southern husbands as an example indicates that median actual expenditures for clothing tended to be approximately 75 percent of the estimated standards of adequacy, a rather substantial discrepancy. If we assume that this discrepancy is due to error, we must also assume that clothing prices were at least one-fourth lower in the years from 1888 through 1890 than in 1908, that estimated standards of adequacy were too high by a margin of one-fourth, that families were able to supplement clothing purchases by a margin of one-third; or else we can make some combination of the three assumptions. In the case of Northern wives as a further example, we would need to assume that prices were at least one-third lower in the years 1888 through 1890, that the estimated standards are too high by one-third, that the clothing of wives was supplemented by one-half, or make some combination of the three assumptions to account for the discrepancies in terms of error.

These assumptions clearly involve rather large margins for error. We should recall, moreover, that even if we made adjustments of this sort to compensate for assumed error, fully half of the families would still remain below an adjusted standard of adequacy. Even larger adjustments would be required if we wished to bring a larger proportion, say 75 percent, up to the standard of adequacy. In that case it would be necessary to assume that actual prices were 50 percent lower than the estimates used in the preceding tables; that the standard of adequacy was really half that given in tables 6.3 and 6.4; that families were able to double their clothing through supplementary means; or, again, some combination of the three.

The question is, are margins of error of this magnitude plausible? If our answer is no, the conclusion follows that for a large but not precisely known portion of the families, clothing was not adequate in terms of a reasonable standard.

INCOME AND FAMILY SPENDING

We can think of family spending as involving choices subject to constraints. One set of constraints has to do with the commodities available in the marketplace and their prices. A further set involves the amounts of money available. Below some level of income, and without supplementary resources, choice can be imagined as sharply constrained or as virtually absent. Income must be spent primarily for necessities. People are, of course, not always totally rational and provident in their spending, and it is likely that most people even at the lowest level of income manage an occasional luxury. Luxuries must come, however, at the cost of less adequate food, shelter, or clothing, and while some choice remains even at the lowest income levels—as, for example, between alternative food commodities—preference must usually be for the least expensive. It is this consideration that dictated use of coarser grades of clothing in constructing the clothing standards used above.

We can see, of course, that as income increases in relation to needs, choice also increases. At higher levels of income more and better food, more and higher quality clothing, better housing, and so on can be afforded. At the same time, as the demands of necessities are increasingly satisfied, income can be spent for discretionary purposes. We are back to Engel's Laws discussed in chapter 3. We can see that the proportion of income spent on necessities is a crude indicator of standard of living and that the choices made in spending discretionary income are clues to values and preferences.

We can see the first of these relationships by comparing the median percentage of family income spent on necessities for each per capita income quartile. Comparison indicates that families in the lowest per capita income quartile spent a median of approximately 90 percent of income on food, clothing, and housing; those in the second quartile, approximately 84 percent; in the third quartile, 77 percent; and in the fourth quartile, approximately 67 percent. Clearly, and as we expected, the greater the income, the lower the proportion of income spent on the combination of food, clothing, and housing and the more that was left to spend for other purposes.

The next question is how did families choose to spend "surplus" income when their income was sufficient to meet the requirements of necessities? We can address this question by employing the tools of regression and correlation introduced in chapter 5. Table 6.5 gives the correlation and regression coefficients obtained by regressing the percentages of income spent for food, clothing, housing, discretionary purposes, sickness and death, and the end-of-year financial position of the families on per capita income.

To interpret the coefficients in table 6.5, we must keep the relationships of concern in mind. Higher income families tended to spend more for most purposes than lower income families. The higher the income, the greater the amounts of money spent for most purposes. On the other hand, higher

Table 6.5
Correlation and Regression of Percentage of Family Income Spent for Specific Purposes on Per Capita Family Income for All Families, and for Families in the First and Fourth Per Capita Income Quartiles

Table 6.5A: Correlation Coefficients

	All Families	Families in Lowest Per Capita Income Quartile	Families in Highest Per Capita Income Quartile
Percentage of Income Spent on:			
Food	-.58	-.26	-.45
Housing	-.14	-.17	-.09
Clothing	-.28	-.11	-.19
Sickness and Death	-.12	-.11	-.03
Discretionary Purposes	.15	.08	.08
End-of-Year Surplus or Deficit	.52	.31	.34

Table 6.5B: Regression Coefficients

Food	-.098	-.236	-.060
Housing	-.016	-.110	-.014
Clothing	-.024	-.057	-.015
Sickness and Death	-.007	-.033	-.002
Discretionary Purposes	+.009	+.021	+.006
End-of-Year Surplus or Deficit	+.135	+.436	+.083

income families also tended to spend lower percentages of their income for many purposes, such as necessities, than lower income families; the higher the income the lower the percentages of income spent for food and other necessities. Decline in the percentage of income spent for particular purposes in relation to higher per capita income would be reflected in negative regression and correlation coefficients; increase in the percentages of income spent for particular purposes in relation to higher income would be reflected in positive coefficients.

The size of the correlation and regression coefficients reflects the consistency and magnitude of these relationships. A low correlation coefficient indicates that the relationship with per capita income is relatively inconsistent (or weak), and a higher coefficient indicates that the relationship is more consistent (or stronger). A low regression coefficient indicates a small difference in the percentage of income spent for the given purpose in relation to per capita income and a higher coefficient a larger difference.

Returning to table 6.5 we can see that the signs are consistently in the directions we expected. The signs are negative for the percentages of income spent on food, clothing, housing, sickness, and death, but positive for discretionary spending and the surplus or deficit positions of the families. In other words, the higher the per capita family income, the lower the percentages of income spent for food, clothing, housing, sickness, and death. In contrast, the higher the per capita income the larger the percentage of income used for discretionary purposes and to improve the financial positions of the families. At higher levels of income, families tended to divert spending from necessities to saving and other discretionary purposes.

The strongest relations appear where spending for food and the surplus and deficit measure are concerned. In both cases, the correlation coefficients are moderately high indicating a relatively strong and reasonably consistent relationship. The amount of difference in spending for food and in the financial situation of the families indicated by the regression coefficients is also greater. On the average, with each dollar of greater per capita income, spending for food was one-tenth of a percent of income less, for each ten dollars of additional income spending for food tended to be one percent less, and for each $100, ten percent less.

Again on the average, with each dollar of additional per capita income the end-of-year family deficits or surpluses (calculated as percentages of total income) tended to improve by approximately fourteen one-hundredths (.135) of a percent of income. Thus for each dollar of additional per capita income, the end-of-year financial position improved by .135 percent of income, for each ten dollars of additional income by 1.35 percent, and so on. Where the other three variables are concerned, the correlation and regression coefficients are lower. We can see, in other words, that change in these variables in relation to per capita income was neither as large nor as consistent as of spending for food or the size of family surpluses and deficits.

We can see that table 6.5 is compatible with several generalizations. The proportion of income spent for necessities declines in relation to income. The rate of decline, however, is lower and less consistent in the case of clothing, housing, sickness and death than in the case of food. This pattern is consistent with the view that at higher income levels the families did not choose, or were unable, to reduce the percentage of income spent for clothing, housing, sickness and death in the same degree as the percentage of income spent for food.

As the demands of necessities decreased, spending for discretionary purposes increased. We do not, however, see evidence of large diversions of surplus income to discretionary spending. The correlation and regression coefficients are much lower in the case of discretionary spending than in the case of the end-of-year deficit and surplus measure. That data suggest, in other words, that when income was sufficient to support necessities, the families chose to reduce deficits or to save rather than to spend for other discretionary purposes.

We must exercise care in interpreting the coefficients in table 6.5 and entertain reservations in accepting these conclusions. In the first place, we must remember that the values involved are percentages and not dollars and cents. Secondly, we must also consider the frailties of the measures. The measure of discretionary spending is not entirely adequate. If we examined the specific components we might find different results. It is also clear that some of the spending for food and other necessities was actually discretionary in nature.

A third qualification is more complicated. We can recognize that the relationship between per capita income and the several spending measures was not the same at all levels of income. As an example, the regression coefficient for percentage of income spent for food is $-.24$ ($r = -.26$) for families in the lowest per capita income quartile but only $-.06$ ($r = -.45$) for families in the highest quartile. The rate of decline in proportionate food expenditures among families in the highest quartile was lower, in other words, than among families in the lowest quartile. This nonlinear relationship is as would be expected. The percentage of income spent on food cannot decline to zero. No matter how high the income, food must be purchased, and the rate of decline in the percentage of income spent on food must tend to diminish at higher income levels.

We can see the same pattern appears where improvement of family financial situations is concerned. Among families in the lowest per capita income quartile the regression coefficient for the relationship between per capita income and the percentage of income used to improve financial situations is +.44 (r = +.31). The corresponding coefficient for families in the highest per capita income quartile is +.08 (r = .34). Again, the pattern is as we would expect. The proportion of income saved in relation to income cannot increase to 100 percent. Some money must always be spent rather than saved no matter how high the income. Thus the rate of increase in percentage of income saved must decline at higher levels of income. (Such relationships can also be referred to as *asymptotic*.)

CONCLUSIONS AND QUALIFICATIONS

The standard of adequate clothing employed in this chapter provides an indication of the items and the number of items of clothing that could be acquired at a given level of expenditure. When we examine that standard (table 6.3) we can see that above the level of spending indicated, families could enjoy a better standard of dress; below that level of spending the level of dress was poorer. We can question the standards given in table 6.3 and recalculated in table 6.4. If prices were significantly lower than those used in calculating these standards, or if families were able to supplement purchased clothing with clothing from other sources, particularly home sewing, then the families would have been able to enjoy better dress than the cost comparisons indicate.

Even so, we will find it instructive to accept the standards at face value for the moment, use them to gain a better view of the way people dressed at the time, and compare their dress with the standards of our own time. We can assume that more families were able to meet the standards reflected in tables 6.3 and 6.4 than the cost comparisons indicate. We must also assume, however, that the clothing of many families fell below, often well below, these standards. It is useful, therefore, to ponder some of the components of the standard.

We can begin by asking, as an example, whether boys aged ten to thirteen really needed suits. If income was insufficient to support the clothing standard given in table 6.3, would a boy of this age be deprived if he did not have a suit. Here we should recall that even boys in these days sometimes went to church and were required to attend special occasions at school and elsewhere. We should also recall that while boys may be indifferent to appearance, their parents are usually not. As a further example, the adequacy of six pairs of stockings and two sets of underwear for the year might be considered, with thought given to our own experience. At a minimum, we should ponder the amount of mending, patching, and darning that would be required to keep these items of clothing in serviceable condition.

One result of such considerations is to suggest ways that clothing purchases could have been reduced if income was insufficient. A further result would be the conclusion that even at best the clothing standards given in table 6.3 are below our own standards. When we recall that the clothing of a large number of families did not meet this standard, a picture of inadequate clothing follows.

The same conclusions result from the other comparisons in this chapter. While we must keep the limitations of our measures clearly in mind, it remains the case that the large majority of family income went to support food, housing, clothing, and the costs of sickness and death. Relatively little was left over for savings, to support vacations and recreation, books, and newspapers, or for other discretionary purposes.

TO THE READER

This section has two primary goals. One is to look at the dress of more specific groups of families. The second goal involves the "family life cycle" hypothesis that we formulated at the beginning of this chapter and suggested as a possible explanation of differences in family income and well-being.

Our first goal involves three subgoals: (1) an improved view of the nature of clothing among textile workers and their families; (2) a better assessment of the impact of differences in income upon family dress; and (3) a more critical evaluation of the standards of clothing adequacy given in table 6.3 and of the estimates, assumptions, and inferences upon which that standard rests. For this purpose table 6.6 gives median expenditures for higher and lower income families in the same eight regional and nationality groups used in earlier chapters. The first panel of the table gives median expenditures for clothing for the 50 percent of the families with per capita income levels below the median for the entire set of families. The second panel gives the same information for families with per capita income above the median for the entire group of families. We must group the families in this fashion because the number of families in some regional and nationality groups is too small to permit comparison of smaller income groups. Families with income from paying boarders are again excluded. Expenditures for children's clothing are calculated on a per capita basis.

A number of the differences and distributions that appear in the table merit further thought and consideration. At both levels of income and in all groups, for example, expenditures for clothing for wives appear lower, and often very substantially lower, than expenditures for husbands. We should ask why that should be and whether the same differences would appear in the modern day. A little paper and pencil calculation allows comparison of the ratio of expenditures for wives to expenditures for husbands at low income with the ratio at higher income levels. The question is whether wives tended to "catch up" with husbands as income increased. It is clear that per capita expenditures for children's clothing compare much more favorably with expenditures for clothing for wives and husbands among the higher income families than among lower income families. Once again, thought should be given to possible reasons for this difference.

Comparison of spending levels from one income and regional and nationality group to the other is all well and good. What we would really like to know is how the several groups actually differed in dress, or, in other words, what they actually chose to purchase. As noted above, the data do not allow us to estimate this information. Combined with the estimated standards

Table 6.6
Median Actual Clothing Expenditure of Families in
Two Per Capita Income Categories by Region and Nationality Group

Families With Per Capita Income Below Median Per Capita Income for All Families

	Median Clothing Expenditures			
	Husband	Wife	Per Child	Number of Families
Northern Native Stock	$21.50	$17.10	$11.90	258
Northern French Canadians	15.50	9.30	8.40	101
Northern Canadians	17.50	10.30	9.10	43
Northern British	19.40	11.20	11.10	141
Northern Irish	19.10	11.60	12.80	146
Northern Continental Europeans	15.70	12.50	10.00	80
Border State Native Stock	18.00	9.20	12.60	90
Southern Native Stock	19.20	11.40	11.00	286

Families With Per Capita Income Above Median Per Capita Income for All Families

	Husband	Wife	Per Child	Number of Families
Northern Native Stock	$25.20	$24.20	$16.60	388
Northern French Canadians	9.20	13.80	14.10	65
Northern Canadians	26.70	14.00	24.00	28
Northern British	27.70	20.00	22.00	212
Northern Irish	26.50	19.30	29.10	169
Northern Continental Europeans	25.50	18.30	17.50	99
Border State Native Stock	20.70	14.40	19.30	64
Southern Native Stock	27.70	19.80	19.00	122

given in table 6.3, the data do provide a basis for tentative estimates of what families could have purchased at differing income levels. In this indirect way, we can gain a sense of the characteristics of family clothing and how the groups tended to differ in clothing.

To make these estimates tables 6.7A and B can be used for working purposes. Table 6.7A provides (from table 6.3) for the South the expenditure levels for particular items of clothing required to clothe individuals at a

Table 6.7A
Adjusted Family Clothing Budgets for Southern
Families with Per Capita Income Below and Above
Median Per Capita Income

		Below Median Income:		Above Median Income:	
Husband					
	Price	Number of Items	Cost	Number of Items	Cost
Suit	$8.00				
Overcoat	(NA)				
Trousers (pair)	1.00				
Light Shirt	1.00				
Colored Shirt	.25				
Overalls	.75				
Winter Underwear	(NA)				
Summer Underwear	1.00				
Shoes (pair)	2.34				
Stockings	.10				
Hats	.50				
Necktie	.25				
Suspenders	.25				
Handkerchiefs	.10				
Total Costs					
Wife					
Suit	5.75				
Coat	(NA)				
Waist (wool)	(NA)				
Skirt (wool)	(NA)				
Gingham or Calico Dresses	.75				
Petticoats	.36				
Drawers	.125				
Undershirts	.25				
Hats or Head Coverings	1.00				
Stockings	.25				
Gingham Aprons	.25				
Shoes (pairs)	1.50				
Handkerchiefs	.05				
Gloves (pair)	.50				
Calico Waists	.26				
Calico or Duck Skirts	.40				
Total Costs					

level above an estimated "poverty line." Table 6.7B provides the same information for the Northern states. Put differently and as discussed above, these are the levels of expenditure estimated as required to maintain a "decent" standard of dress.

Table 6.7A and B, and the median actual expenditures given in table 6.6, should be used to compare the several groups, improve our understanding of the impact of differences in income on standards of dress, and gain a

Table 6.7A (continued)

		Below Median Income:			Above Median Income:	
	Price	Number of Items	Cost		Number of Items	Cost
Son						
Suit	3.50					
Overcoat	(NA)					
Trousers	.50					
Shirts	.30					
Winter Underwear	.50					
Summer Underwear	.50					
Hat	.50					
Suspenders	.25					
Stockings (pair)	.34					
Shoes	1.50		————			————
Total Costs						
Daughter						
Wool Dress	(NA)					
Gingham Dress	.62					
Coat	(NA)					
Cotton Petticoats	.25					
Drawers	.125					
Winter Undershirts	.25					
Hats	1.00					
Stockings	.25					
Mittens	(NA)					
Shoes (pairs)	2.00					
Ribbons	(NA)					
Total Costs	$14.35		————			————
Total Costs for Family						

(NA) Not ascertained or not applicable.

better view of how the families actually dressed. For this purpose, a particular regional and nationality group should be selected. One task is to reduce
the items of clothing, and the number of items, given in tables 6.7A or B to
levels that could be supported at the median levels of actual expenditures
for that group as given in table 6.6. A second task is to adjust the items of
clothing, and the number of items, to levels supportable at the median
levels of actual expenditures by higher income families in this group. Again,

Table 6.7B
Adjusted Family Clothing Budgets for Northern Families with
Per Capita Income Below and Above Median Per Capita Income

		Below Median Income:		Above Median Income:	
Husband					
	Price	Number of Items	Cost	Number of Items	Cost
Suit	$8.00				
Overcoat	4.00				
Trousers (pair)	1.50				
Light Shirt	1.00				
Colored Shirt	.25				
Overalls	.50				
Winter Underwear	1.00				
Summer Underwear	1.00				
Shoes (pair)	2.34				
Stockings	.10				
Hats	.50				
Necktie	.50				
Suspenders	.25				
Handkerchiefs	.10				
Total Costs			——		——

Wife					
Suit	(NA)				
Coat	1.60				
Waist (wool)	6.25				
Skirt (wool)	.25				
Gingham or Calico Dresses	.95				
Petticoats	.60				
Drawers	.20				
Undershirts	.35				
Hats or Head Coverings	1.00				
Stockings	.34				
Gingham Aprons	(NA)				
Shoes (pairs)	1.50				
Handkerchiefs	.67				
Gloves (pair)	.50				
Calico Waists	.18				
Calico or Duck Skirts	.90				
Total Costs			——		——

table 6.6 can be used to identify the income levels of the group in question. Note that in the case of some higher income groups, this will also entail reductions in clothing.

In carrying out this work several additional requirements should be noted. Since the medians given for children are based upon per capita expenditures, the reduced (or increased) clothing purchases for children should be for a single child. Because costs of meeting the estimated stan-

Table 6.7B (continued)

	Below Median Income:			Above Median Income:	
	Price	Number of Items	Cost	Number of Items	Cost
Son					
Suit	4.00				
Overcoat	3.00				
Trousers	.75				
Shirts	.30				
Winter Underwear	1.00				
Summer Underwear	1.00				
Hat	.50				
Suspenders	.25				
Stockings (pair)	.42				
Shoes	2.00		___		___
Total Costs					
Daughter					
Wool Dress	2.00				
Gingham Dress	.61				
Coat	2.00				
Cotton Petticoats	.40				
Drawers	.125				
Winter Undershirts	.25				
Hats	.50				
Stockings	.25				
Mittens	.25				
Shoes (pairs)	2.50				
Ribbons	(NA)		___		___
Total Costs					
Total Costs for Family					

(NA) Not ascertained or not applicable.

dards of adequacy for female children are lower than for male children, a family will appear somewhat better off if a female child is assumed and worse off if a male child is assumed. If Southern or Border State families are selected for consideration, table 6.7A, which gives the Southern standard, should be used. Obviously, for Northern groups, table 6.7B, is indicated.

Note that we cannot "cannibalize" expenditures by reducing clothing more sharply for some family members, as children, in order to allow more clothing for others. The medians in table 6.6 are actual expenditures. On the other hand, estimates can be made of possible augmentation of family clothing through home sewing, reuse of material such as flour sacks, and the like.

While we should take possible augmentations of family clothing of this sort into consideration, completion of our task will be most simple if it is initially assumed that all family clothing was purchased at the prices indicated in table 6.7A and B. Estimates made on this basis can than be adjusted upward using estimates of possible augmentations.

Explicit thought should be given to the assumptions made in adjusting family clothing purchases to correspond to different levels of actual expenditures. Should we take some items as less necessary than others and why? If we assume that some items were made at home, which items, how many, why these items, and the estimated saving to the family should be explicitly considered. As a final step, subjective evaluations of the adjusted family clothing purchases should be made: how well did the families dress, how did their dress compare with the standards of today, and how adequate are the standards given in table 6.3 and 6.7A and 6.7B? Are they realistic or unrealistic, too high, too low, and why?

Our second goal in this section is to confront more directly the "family life cycle" hypothesis sketched at the beginning of this chapter. We should understand to start with that it will be possible only to increase or decrease confidence in the plausibility of the formulation. We will not be able to definitively support or refute the formulation.

We will also recognize that the family life cycle formulation cannot be explored as originally stated. The formulation suggests, however, a series of "operational" hypotheses that can be tested using the data collection. It will be recognized that some of the sub-hypotheses below follow more necessarily from the original formulation than others, and that still others could be derived from them.

If the formulation is valid:

1. We would expect that husbands and wives in higher per capita income families would tend to be older than in lower income

families. We would not expect that husbands and wives in higher income families would be younger than in lower income families.

2. We would expect that husbands in higher per capita income families would have higher earnings than husbands in lower income families. The reverse would not be expected.

3. We would expect that higher per capita income families would include fewer children than lower income families. The opposite tendency would refute the hypothesis.

4. We would expect that higher per capita income families would be more heavily dependent upon the earnings of husbands than lower income families.

We already have some information bearing upon these propositions for the families taken as a group. In table 6.1, for example, families in the highest per capita income quartile appear as including fewer children than families in the lower quartiles. Differences between the quartiles in expenditures for clothing for family members (table 6.2) also suggest the smaller size of higher per capita income families. On the other hand, comparison of the median age of husbands from one per capita income quartile to the next (table 6.1) does not provide consistent support for the hypothesis.

It is possible, however, that by treating the entire set of families as a group without regard to region of residence or nationality we have concealed differences that might or might not refute or support the original hypothesis. To partially rectify this problem table 6.8 compares high and low income families in terms of the median age of husbands, median income of husbands, median number of children, and the median percentage of family income derived from the earnings of husbands. The table employs the same income groupings and regional and nationality categories as table 6.6.

The question is, does the table confirm or refute the hypothesis? The best answer is probably neither. For some groups the data seem reasonably compatible with the general hypothesis and with some of the subhypotheses. For others the pattern is inconsistent and for still other groups the pattern is almost the opposite of that predicted by the hypothesis and subhypotheses. Our next question is, what explains this state of affairs? Why do the data consistently fail either to confirm or to refute the hypotheses?

Two responses will immediately come to mind. One is essentially methodological. The income groupings are broad, and it is possible they may conceal divergent tendencies within the economic categories. The median is also a rather blunt instrument for the purposes of the table. Its use may obscure rather than reveal patterns that would more convincingly refute or confirm the hypotheses.

Table 6.8
Characteristics of High and Low Per Capita Incomee Families by Income Level and Regional and Nationality Group

	Median Husband's Age		Median Husband's Income		Median Number of Children		Median % of Income from Husband	
	Lowest Income	Highest Income	Lowest Income	Highest Income	Lowest Income	Highest Income	Lowest Income	Highest Income
Northern Native Stock	34.9	37.1	$432.0	$524.40	2.8	0.8%	97.7%	98.4%
Northern French Canadians	35.4	35.5	350.3	375.5	3.8	1.3	65.6	64.8
Northern Canadians	33.9	43.0	369.5	367.0	3.8	2.0	94.3	34.0
Northern British	37.8	42.3	434.0	490.0	3.1	1.2	93.5	73.6
Northern Irish	40.6	44.9	342.0	397.4	4.0	1.7	92.3	58.0
Northern Continental Europeans	37.3	40.5	358.0	464.92	3.0	1.3	89.0	74.3
Border State Native Stock	40.5	39.0	307.0	431.0	3.6	0.8	61.5	85.0
Southern Native Stock	38.1	32.0	249.1	373.09	2.9	0.7	52.7	72.0

The second response is of a different order. We were probably not naive enough to believe that the life cycle formulation would explain all differences in the income and living condition of all families and groups. Other factors also enter in. We know that in our own day some people begin at low levels of income and poor living conditions and across their life span gradually "work up" to higher income and better living conditions. We know as well that some people begin at higher levels than others and either remain there or move to still higher levels. Others begin at low levels and tend to remain there. We know, in other words, that the life experience is not the same for all individuals. We know that groups of individuals and families differ in these same respects. Minority groups and women in our own time have less opportunity to work up and improve their conditions than do white males. We would expect that similar factors and differences in opportunity also existed and had similar consequence in the late nineteenth century.

These considerations lead to still different questions. What other factors in addition to experience across the life span are likely to have affected the income and living conditions of particular families and groups of families? Does table 6.8 suggest that some groups may have enjoyed greater opportunity than others or that the factors that affected the income and living conditions of some groups were different than those that affected others?

— 7 —
FAMILY DIETS

We are concerned here with the type, quantity, and quality of food consumed by textile workers and their families and with the relationship between food consumption on the one hand, and income and the size and composition of the families on the other. To put the matter a little differently, we are concerned with what the families ate, how well they ate, and what they chose to eat when they had a choice.

The significance of these issues requires little explanation. We would all agree that for most of us the nature, quantity, and quality of food consumed are fundamental components of life and basic determinants of the quality of life. We need only note in passing the central importance of nutrition and diet to health, vigor, functional capacity, the development of children, longevity, and to the sense of a "good" as opposed to an unsatisfactory life.

For the families of concern here these issues are of particular significance. We observed in chapter 3 (table 3.1) that approximately 42 percent of the total income of these families went to purchase food. Among families in the lowest per capita income quartile, slightly over 50 percent of total income was spent on food; even among families in the highest income quartile spending for food accounted for almost one-third of total income. For these families, food constituted the largest single expense and the central item in family budgets. While questions of food consumption are of central intrinsic importance, they also force us to give systematic consideration to problems of error, distortion, and inference.

SPENDING FOR FOOD

Our first question concerns the staple commodities in family diets. In other words, what commodities were consumed by most or all of the families? One way to begin to address this question is to tabulate the percentage of families that indicated they had purchased each of the 21 food commodities reflected in the source collection. This information is given in table 7.1. We might agree that commodities which most families reported purchasing were staples in family diets, while commodities that few families purchased were not. By classifying families in terms of per capita income, we gain a preliminary notion of differences in diets in relation to income.

Table 7.1 might lead us to conclude that poultry, rice, cheese (and possibly fish) were not staple components in family diets. The percentage of families that reported purchasing these commodities is relatively low. The percentage of families with expenditures for fish, however, increases from the lowest to the highest per capita income quartile. We might take this

Table 7.1
**Percentage of Families Reporting Purchases of Categories
of Food Commodities by Per Capita Income Quartiles***

Families with Income In:

	First Quartile	Second Quartile	Third Quartile	Fourth Quartile
Beef	51.4%	45.0%	47.6%	45.4%
Hog	75.4	60.7	59.5	51.2
Meat	82.2	87.6	89.9	91.8
Eggs	81.7	85.1	83.6	82.0
Lard	88.4	91.6	90.1	86.9
Butter	91.9	95.2	95.1	93.9
Tea	60.2	76.1	82.0	85.9
Coffee	77.5	81.9	79.8	83.7
Sugar	98.8	98.1	98.6	96.1
Molasses	64.6	60.2	55.3	50.2
Potatoes	93.3	94.9	95.8	92.0
Poultry	9.9	8.5	6.8	7.8
Fish	50.9	63.9	64.6	67.2
Milk	77.1	85.8	88.0	89.8
Flour /Meal	98.9	99.7	98.1	95.7
Bread	39.4	44.3	48.3	46.4
Rice	25.0	18.1	17.1	11.7
Cheese	40.8	41.7	36.5	33.2
Fruit	55.5	71.6	72.8	71.6
Vinegar, Pickles, Condiments	24.5	25.8	21.3	21.1
Vegetables	92.4	91.8	88.0	84.4
Other	98.2	98.6	97.7	98.1

* Families with income from boarders are excluded.

increase as indicating choices that could be made at higher income levels, or as merely a reflection of regional variations in the availability of fish. Flour and meal were apparently staple elements of family diets at all income levels, and it appears that most families baked rather than purchased bread. Surprisingly the percentages of families with expenditures for condiments is small. Since the prices of these commodities were low, as suggested by the letter reproduced in chapter 1, we can suspect that this pattern is a result of what we might call "accounting error." Because prices were low and expenditures small, family members may have been less able to recall how much they spent during the year for these commodities.

The table also suggests the presence of "substitution effects." We can surmise that when income permitted, families tended to substitute food commodities that they preferred for those commodities that they found less desirable. The percentage of families with expenditures for pork decreases across the income quartiles. In contrast, the percentage of families with expenditures for meat increases. The suggestion is that other meats were preferred and were substituted for pork among higher income families.

Contrary to what we might have expected differences in beef consumption between income categories do not consistently follow this pattern. At the risk of rationalizing the data, we might again suspect accounting error as the source of this apparent inconsistency. At first glance, we might take the category "meat (not specified)" to include meats, such as mutton, other than beef and pork. The magnitude of expenditures in this category makes such a supposition unlikely. A more plausible assumption is that this is again an instance in which families, as would be true of many of us today, could not account in detail for the specific types of meat that they purchased but could estimate only total meats purchased. Under this assumption, the "meat" category would include not only mutton, but beef and perhaps pork as well.

We can also see other substitution patterns, but in some cases less clearly. The data are compatible with the view, for example, that sugar was preferred to molasses and was substituted for molasses as a sweetener at higher income levels. Similarly, tea was seemingly preferred to coffee, and meat products other than pork were preferred to such starchy foods as flour, meal and potatoes.

It is no surprise that higher income families were able to enjoy more varied and desirable, and perhaps more nutritious and healthful, foods than lower income families. The reasons for qualifying our conclusions about health and nutrition will be obvious. Diets that include larger amounts of sugar, tea, and coffee are not necessarily superior in terms of health and nutrition to diets in which these components are smaller. Similarly, the "better" cuts of meats are not always nutritionally superior to the "poorer" ones. Examination of family diets suggests variations in tastes and preferences as well as the food preferences of the time. The consequences of these variations for health and nutrition is a different question.

FOOD CONSUMPTION

Table 7.1 gives us a first indication of the staple components of family diets and suggests foods that were preferred and consumed when income permitted or foregone when income was insufficient. However plausible, we must subject these generalizations to question. Variation in the composition of families has not been taken into account, and the amounts of commodities purchased and consumed have not been examined directly. Either of these omissions could yield erroneous conclusions.

To estimate food consumption we must resort to rather laborious calculations. The resulting estimates depend for their validity on several assumptions. The source collection most consistently gives the amounts of money reported as spent by the families for the various food categories. To convert amounts spent into amounts purchased and consumed, we have employed the information on commodity prices provided by the so called "Aldrich Report" published in 1892. This report was prepared by the Commissioner of Labor for the U.S. Senate Committee on Finance, and gives for different cities the prices in 1889–1891 for a wide range of food commodities including most of those given in our source collection.[1] By dividing the amounts spent by the families for the commodities by the estimated prices of the commodities as derived from the Aldrich Report, we can estimate the amount of most commodities purchased by the families.

Use of the Aldrich Report in this fashion involves, however, a number of complexities. In most cases the Report gives the prices for several specific commodities within the general categories employed in the data collection. In the case of beef, for example, the Report gives prices for "canned corned beef" and "roasting cuts." We have used "roasting cuts" for our "beef" commodity. It will be recognized that a "roasting cut" is neither the best nor the worst cut of beef. It is almost certain that families sometimes, perhaps often, purchased both cheaper and more expensive cuts of beef, so that we have underestimated some and overestimated other amounts of beef purchased and consumed by families. Since some bought poorer cuts at lower prices, they were able to purchase more beef than our estimates indicate. Of course, the reverse is also true.

Other commodities included in the source collection present additional difficulties. The Report gives no prices for the category "meat (not specified)" that is included in the source collection. To estimate prices for this generic commodity we have used the information provided for those fami-

Table 7.2

Estimated Unit Prices for Food Commodities, by Region*

Commodity	Unit	New England	Middle Atlantic	Border States	South
Beef	pound	$0.16	$0.16	$0.11	$0.12
Hog	pound	0.13	0.13	0.09	0.11
Meats	pound	0.12	0.12	0.11	0.08
Eggs	dozen	0.21	0.21	0.15	0.16
Lard	pound	0.10	0.10	0.08	0.09
Butter	pound	0.26	0.26	0.21	0.26
Tea	pound	0.52	0.52	0.58	0.56
Coffee	pound	0.23	0.23	0.22	0.24
Sugar	pound	0.09	0.09	0.08	0.10
Molasses	gallon	0.59	0.59	0.53	0.55
Potatoes	bushel	0.96	0.96	1.03	1.30
Poultry	pound	0.19	0.19	0.16	0.14
Milk	quart	0.06	0.06	0.07	0.09
Flour	pound	0.04	0.04	0.03	0.03
Bread	loaf	0.06	0.06	0.06	0.06
Fish	pound	0.14	0.14	0.13	0.13
Rice	pound	0.09	0.09	0.08	0.07
Cheese	pound	0.16	0.15	0.18	0.18

*Regions include the following states:

New England	Middle Atlantic	South	Border
Connecticut	Delaware	Virginia	Kentucky
Maine	New Jersey	Alabama	Maryland
Massachusetts	New York	Georgia	Tennessee
New Hampshire	Pennsylvania	Louisiana	
Rhode Island		Mississippi	
		North Carolina	
		South Carolina	

lies that reported both the amounts spent for and the amounts of "meat" purchased. By dividing amounts spent by amounts reported as purchased, we have estimated the amounts of "meat" consumed by the families.

Through these procedures we can derive estimates of the prices of 18 of the 21 food commodities given in the collection. These prices are given in table 7.2. We cannot estimate prices for fruits, vegetables, and condiments, nor can we assess the amounts of these commodities consumed by the families. All three are generic categories; no information is given in the source collection as to which condiments, fruits, and vegetables were purchased; whether fruits and vegetables were fresh, canned, or dried; nor can we take into account the wide seasonal, regional, and local variations in prices and consumption. Therefore, any estimates of prices and consumption of these commodities would be highly tenuous.

In the case of several other food categories, similar but less extreme difficulties are present. As in the case of beef, the prices of a number of other commodities are averages. Use of these price estimates to determine amounts consumed will therefore not reflect variations in quality, and the estimates will depart from actual amounts purchased in ways and degrees that we cannot fully assess. A little reflection will suggest that this means our estimates will tend to be less reliable for assessing the absolute quality of diets and more reliable for comparing the consumption patterns of different groups of families.

We could easily divide estimated family food consumption by the number of members in families to determine food consumption per person (per capita food consumption). But this approach would effectively treat all members of families as the same and impose the same demands on family food budgets. The underlying assumption would be unrealistic. We would not assume that infants, for example, would have the same food requirements and impose the same burdens on family income as adults.

Naturally, we would prefer to weight individual family members in terms of their presumed food requirements in order to take into account differences in the size of families as well as in the age and sex of family members. Unfortunately, we have no very good means to do so. The data provide no information that is relevant directly, and it is certain that the food costs associated with comparable family members varied from one family to the next. It would be hard to believe, for example, that there was no variation in the household and cooking practices of families and, hence, no variation in individual food costs from one family to the next. Similarly, the food requirements of individuals employed in more strenuous occupations would be greater than those employed in less strenuous pursuits. The best that we could expect of any weighting scheme is an approximation of actual differences in individual food requirements.

As it happens, we do have the basis for a rudimentary weighting system of this sort. As part of the same investigation that produced the data collection used here, the office of the Commissioner of Labor examined and compared the expenditure patterns and living costs of an extended number of families employed in the iron and steel industry. One of the products of this examination was a scale, or index, intended to reflect "the potential capacity for consuming food of the different members of families." (This scale of "consuming power" is published in the *Sixth Annual Report of the Commissioner of Labor* for 1890, pp. 618–619.)

Converted to decimal fractions, the scale weights husbands as 1 unit, wives and children of 11–14 years of age at .9 units, children of 7–10 at .75, those of age 4–6 at .4, and those under three years of age at .15. In the examination families with children over 14 were excluded from consideration. To compensate for this exclusion we have assumed that male children over fourteen would have the same weight as husbands (1) and that female children over fourteen would have the same weight as wives (.9). The relatively small number of other and unidentified individuals residing with families (non paying boarders, and so on) are weighted as .95 (the average of one adult male and one adult female).

We can use this scale to create a measure of family food consumption that is intended to reflect both the number of people in families and their age and sex. To do so, family members of different ages and sexes are multiplied by the fractions indicated above. The sum of the result, "weighted family size," is then divided into estimated total family consumption of each of the food commodities to create a measure of "family weighted" food consumption. The explicit assumptions that women over fourteen had nine-tenths the food requirements and costs of males of the same age, that the food costs of children of four through six were four-tenths those of males of fourteen or older, and so on, should be carefully considered. If we think about it, we might conceptualize our measure in terms of "average" families taking into account the number, age, and sex of family members.

These procedures are used in table 7.3, which gives estimated average yearly consumption of the food commodities per weighted person in families. The families are again grouped in income quartiles, but in this case, using a family weighted measure of income. That is, total family income is divided by the same measure of weighted family size to calculate "family weighted" per capita income. Families that included paying boarders are excluded.

If we convert the estimates in the table to a weekly basis, we can see that the "average" family member in the lowest income quartile consumed per week, as examples, approximately three-fourths of a quart of milk, eight-tenths of a pound of unspecified meats, over six pounds of flour, and so on.

In contrast, "average" family members in the highest income quartile consumed over two quarts of milk, two and a half pounds of unspecified meats,
and almost five and a half pounds of flour per week.

The most striking aspect of table 7.3 is the increase in food consumption
in relation to income. At higher levels of income, family members consumed more of all commodities except pork, rice, and flour and meal. The
differences, however, vary from one commodity to the other. Family members in the highest income quartile consumed approximately two-and-a-half
times the amount of tea, meat and beef, milk and eggs, almost twice as
much butter and sugar, and about one and a third times the amounts of
potatoes and lard as families at the lowest weighted per capita income level.
On the other hand, the highest income families consumed only approximately 90 percent of the amount of flour and meal and two-thirds as much
pork as the lowest income families.

We gain from table 7.3 a clearer view of family consumption patterns
and, perhaps, food preferences. Potatoes, flour, and meal—starchy foods
which were inexpensive in relation to bulk—appear, along with lard, as

Table 7.3
Estimated Food Consumption per Family Member Weighted by Age
and Sex, by Family Weighted Per Capita Income Quartiles*

Families with Family Weighted Per Capita Income In:

	First Quartile	Second Quartile	Third Quartile	Fourth Quartile
Beef	23.2	30.2	37.0	44.6
Hog	37.6	31.2	28.2	23.0
Meat	44.1	76.7	105.6	130.6
Eggs (doz.)	8.1	12.9	15.1	17.7
Lard	16.8	19.0	21.5	22.3
Butter	16.7	25.6	29.8	34.1
Tea	1.9	3.6	4.5	5.4
Coffee	8.0	8.2	8.9	9.6
Sugar	38.6	52.8	63.7	72.4
Molasses (gal.)	1.1	1.0	1.2	1.1
Potatoes (bu.)	2.0	2.9	3.3	3.4
Poultry	0.7	0.8	0.7	1.1
Fish	3.4	8.1	10.9	13.9
Milk (qt.)	40.0	63.3	85.7	111.8
Flour /Meal	314.6	294.0	291.6	283.9
Bread	24.5	35.0	34.5	42.5
Rice	1.8	1.8	1.7	1.2
Cheese	1.6	2.3	2.1	2.2

*This table excludes families with income from paying
boarders and the five families not reporting either the age or gender of some
of their children. All amounts of commodities listed in the table above are
measured in pounds unless otherwise noted beside the name of the commodity.

staple elements of family diets at all income levels. On the other hand, milk, butter, eggs, and meats (except pork) appear as larger elements of family diets at higher income levels than at lower levels. It appears that other food commodities were preferred to pork, flour, and meal. We also might take the relatively lower rate of increase in consumption of potatoes, lard, and poultry in relation to income as indications that these were not preferred foods.

When we control for differences in family size and composition, it appears, as we expected, that higher income families enjoyed better diets than lower income families. They were able to do so, moreover, even though they spent, on average, a lower percentage of their income for food than low income families. The higher income families were able to enjoy a better standard of living in terms of food and also had more of their income left over to save or to improve their living standards in other areas.

These are plausible conclusions, or are they? Systematic thought should be given to possible sources of error and their likely consequences. Is it likely that error characteristic of the data or shortcomings of the estimating procedures could result in over- or underestimates of food consumption? Is it likely that error or the estimating procedures are the actual sources, for example, of the differences in food consumption from one income quartile to the next that appear in table 7.3?

INCOME AND FOOD CONSUMPTION

Both the amounts of commodities and the specific commodities purchased by families varied in relation to income, as we see in table 7.3. However, the approach used in constructing the table masks variation. On the basis of chapter 6 we would also suspect that the relationship between income and consumption of specific commodities might not be constant at all levels of income.

More specifically, we would not expect to find that the amount of food consumed increased at a constant rate across all income levels. We would particularly expect that among families in the lowest income quartile, consumption of food commodities would be positively related to income and that the higher the income, the greater the amounts consumed of most food commodities. Among families in the highest quartile, we might expect to find that this relationship would be less strong, nonexistent, or even negative. To explore these possibilities table 7.4 presents the correlation and regression coefficients for each food commodity obtained by regressing the estimated amounts of commodities consumed by family members on family weighted per capita income.

When we examine the correlations between family weighted income and

Table 7.4
Regression and Correlation Coefficients for Relationship of Family Weighted Per Capita Income to Consumption of Food Commodities*

	All Families ($22.68 - 1,080.00)		Families In: First Quartile of Weighted Per Capita Income ($22.68 - 121.48)		Fourth Quartile of Weighted Per Capita Income ($216.27 - 1,080.00)	
	Correlation Coefficient	Regression Coefficient	Correlation Coefficient	Regression Coefficient	Correlation Coefficient	Regression Coefficient
Beef	.16	+.10	.20	+.36	.06	+.04
Hog	-.12	-.06	-.03	-.06	-.02	-.01
Meat	.38	+.36	.25	+.63	.00	+.00
Eggs (doz.)	.22	+.03	.26	+.12	-.06	-.01
Lard	.11	+.02	.11	+.07	-.08	-.02
Butter	.32	+.06	.31	+.23	.01	+.00
Tea	.29	+.01	.26	+.03	.02	+.00
Coffee	.09	+.01	-.04	-.01	.09	+.01
Sugar	.40	+.13	.35	+.40	.05	+.02
Molasses (gal.)	-.01	-.00	.00	+.00	-.03	+.00
Potatoes (bu.)	.18	+.00	.29	+.02	-.13	-.00
Poultry	.07	+.00	.02	+.00	.09	+.01
Fish	.27	+.04	.23	+.07	-.04	-.01
Milk (qt.)	.42	+.32	.28	+.62	.17	+.16
Flour/Meal	-.02	-.02	-.02	-.08	-.03	-.04
Bread (loaf)	-.08	+.07	.15	+.46	.02	+.02
Rice	-.05	-.00	.05	+.01	-.06	-.00
Cheese	.03	+.00	.22	+.03	-.02	-.00

*This table excludes families with income from paying boarders.
All amounts of commodities listed in the table above are measured in pounds unless otherwise noted.

consumption for all families (the first column) we find that consumption of sugar, milk, meat, and butter is related at a moderate level to family weighted income. We find the same relation in the case of tea and eggs, but the correlations are somewhat weaker. The correlations between income and consumption of lard, beef, potatoes, and pork are weaker still. However, consumption of lard, beef, and potatoes also tended to increase in relation to income while consumption of pork tended to decline. In contrast, consumption of bread, flour, poultry, coffee, and molasses appear as very weakly correlated with income and our best generalization on the basis of the relevant coefficients is that consumption of these commodities was not systematically related to income.

The correlation coefficients are in accord with—or do not contradict—the patterns we observed in table 7.3. In that table, consumption of sugar, milk, meat, butter, lard, beef, and potatoes tended to increase consistently from the lowest to the highest income quartiles while consumption of pork tended to decline. Differences in consumption of flour and meal did not appear as either particularly pronounced or completely consistent, leading us to infer that these commodities tended to be staples at all income levels and that consumption did not fluctuate systematically with income. Similarly, change in consumption of coffee and molasses was not consistent from one income quartile to the next, and most families reported no consumption of fish, poultry, rice, or bakery bread.

The regression coefficients in table 7.4, as we know, can be interpreted straightforwardly as the amount of difference in consumption of the various commodities in relation to differences in income. Across all families, yearly consumption of eggs per weighted family member increased on the average by approximately .03 dozen for each dollar of greater income. Sugar consumption increased by almost one-eighth of a pound for each dollar of greater income. The values are obviously very small and care is needed in their interpretation. We can put the relationship in another way by saying that yearly consumption of unspecified meat commodities, to use another example, increased on the average by 3.6 pounds per weighted family member for each ten dollars of greater weighted per capita income while pork consumption declined .6 pounds for each ten dollars of greater income.

We can also use the coefficients to compare differences in consumption of specific commodities between income quartiles. The correlation coefficients for families in the lowest weighted per capita income quartile follow much the same pattern as those for the entire set of families, although specific values tend to be somewhat lower. The regression coefficients do show some differences. The coefficients for butter, sugar, milk, unspecified meats, and beef are higher in the case of the low income families, suggesting a greater rate of increase in consumption of these commodities in relation to income than for the entire set of families.

The correlation and regression coefficients for families that ranked in the highest weighted income quartile present a substantially different picture. Effectively, the picture is one of no relationship between income and consumption of the various food commodities. Differences in signs can be observed. The signs for eggs, potatoes, lard and molasses are negative for the higher income families but positive both for the entire set of families and for the lowest income families. But the correlation coefficients for the highest income quartile are so low for all commodities that they must be taken as indicating no relation between food consumption and income.

It does appear from table 7.3 that consumption of most commodities was greater among families that ranked in the highest income category than among families in the lower income categories. Within the highest income category, however, food consumption neither increased nor decreased systematically in relation to differences in income. We can recognize that this pattern is in accord with results and discussions in chapter 6.

We can conclude from table 7.4 that the relationship between income and food consumption among the families was not consistent (or constant) at all income levels. Among lower income families consumption of most food commodities was associated with income: the higher the income the greater the amounts of most commodities family members tended to consume. Among higher income families, in contrast, food consumption was apparently unrelated—or even negatively related—to income. Higher income tended not to result in greater food consumption among these families, and consumption of a number of food commodities tended if anything to decline in relation to income, although the tendency was faint.

CONCLUSIONS AND QUALIFICATIONS

Our examination is compatible with several generalizations concerning relationships between income, family size, and food consumption. Higher income families (measuring income as family weighted per capita income) tended to spend less on food in terms both of actual dollar amounts and of proportion of total income than lower income families. Because of differences in family size and composition, however, members of higher income families consumed more of most food commodities than members of lower income families. Food consumption was not consistently related to income across the entire set of families. Among lower income families the relationship tended to be the higher the income the greater the amounts consumed

of most commodities; among higher income families there was little systematic relationship between income and amounts of food consumed.

We can also observe other dietary differences. Flour and meal, potatoes,
bread, lard, and butter were staple components of family diets at all income
levels. At higher income levels, however, meat (except pork), fish, butter,
milk, eggs, sugar and tea were larger elements of family diets than among
lower income families. In other words, starches and fats were apparently
major elements in the diets of most families, but the diets of higher income
families also tended to be higher in protein (and cholesterol) than those of
lower income families. The diets of higher income families were, it appears,
both more nearly suited to their preferences and better in terms of quantity
and, perhaps, quality. Among these families income was sufficient to support better dietary standards and still leave more funds to save or spend for
other purposes.

Taken in total, our examination conveys an impression of inadequate
diets among lower income families. The correlation between weighted per
capita income and amounts of commodities consumed by lower income
families suggests that for these families income was not sufficient to meet
food requirements. Hence, greater income resulted in greater consumption
of most commodities. The absence of such a relation among higher income
families suggests that for these families income was sufficient to meet food
requirements.

TO THE READER

Following upon our examination of food consumption, a logical next step
would be to assess the nutritional character of family diets. We would like
to address such questions as whether some families were malnourished in
any sense, whether they tended to suffer from particular dietary deficien-
cies, and whether or not there were specific elements in their diets that left
them prone to disease or other maladies. Investigation of such questions
might well lead us to additional chains of questions. We might find, for
example, that the diets of many families were similar to those that have
been found in the modern day to be associated with heart disease. If we did
so find, we might next ask why the available statistics, inadequate though
they are, suggest that the incidence of heart disease was lower at the end of
the nineteenth century than it is today.

Nutrition is, of course, a large and complex field. It would be fascinating
to pursue questions such as these, but to attempt to do so here would take
us well beyond the scope of this book. Even so, a little independent library
work would quickly lead the reader to additional information bearing upon
the health and well-being of the families, and of others like them, and might

suggest the presence of endemic diseases and dietary disorders that reduced the quality of life at the time.

Leaving such questions for independent inquiry, we turn here to comparison of more specific groups of families and individuals including both those reflected in the data collection as well as individuals in our own time. Our questions are, again, which groups tended to be best and worst off, in what ways, and what factors help to explain the relative well-being of the families. To make these comparisons, however, will require that we address systematically problems of error, distortion, and omission that could reduce the validity of our comparisons or lead us to misinterpretations and mistaken conclusions. It will be recognized that these problems must also be taken into account while employing library sources to assess the nutritional properties of family diets.

Problems of Error

When we examine any of the preceding tables we will recognize that they are affected by the errors—the departures of recorded values from true values—that are inevitably present in some unknown degree in our data collection, just as would be true of any collection of source material whether historical or contemporary. Because error is unavoidable, it is necessary to invest effort in assessing aspects of its character and likely consequences.

For these purposes it is useful to think of error as consisting of two forms, each with different consequences. As illustrated by our data collection, one form of error is the result of the essentially random mistakes made by family members in reporting consumption, spending, age, and so on, by the officials who recorded, tabulated, and published the information; or in converting the data from tabular to computer-readable form. Error created by mistakes of this sort results in recorded values that are equally likely to be higher or lower than true values. That is, the amounts recorded as spent for pork, for example, are equally likely to be higher or lower than the amounts actually spent.

Error of this sort introduces what amounts to random "noise" but is unlikely to consistently bias the data either upward or downward from true values. A little thought will suggest that the consequence of this type of error is to blur or mask differences between families or groups of families. We can do little about this type of error except recognize that it is always present. We can also understand that to the degree it is present, the true differences or similarities between families are likely to appear less pronounced than they actually were.

The second form of error, usually referred to as bias, has quite different consequences. In this form of error, recorded values tend to be consistently higher (or lower) than the true values. If this form of error is present, family diets, for example, will appear systematically better (or worse), while income will appear higher (or lower), and so on, than was actually true of the families. Similarly, for some groups of families the recorded values can be biased upward from true values while for other groups the recorded values can be systematically biased downward. Thus the appearance of difference is created or enhanced even though no differences really existed or actual differences were smaller than (or even opposite from) the apparent differences.

We can assume that the data bearing upon consumption of specific food commodities included in the source collection are biased in a downward direction if for no other reason than because of the amounts given in the collection as spent for "other food costs." The families, as would be true of families today, were apparently unable to account for all food expenditures in terms of specific commodities. Additional spending over and above accountable spending was simply lumped together in this residual category.

Given this assumption, we could conclude that our assessment of family food consumption is once again a "worst case analysis"—at least in this respect. Given this assumption we could conclude that the families actually consumed more food than is indicated by our estimates of the amounts consumed of specific commodities. Further, and much more risky, assumptions would be (1) that the amounts listed as spent in the "other food costs" category were actually spent for the specific food commodities included in the collection and not for some other commodities, and (2) that the amounts given in this residual category were actually proportionately distributed across the specific food categories and were not in actuality disproportionately spent for some commodities rather than others.

If we were willing to make these assumptions, we could increase the amounts recorded as spent for specific commodities in proportion to the amounts recorded in the residual category and recalculate the estimated food consumption. In this way we could create, by assumption, new and higher estimates of consumption of the specific commodities that compensated for the nature and magnitude of one category of bias that we have assumed to be present in the data collection.

Whether we would be willing to risk these assumptions in the present case is a matter for thought and debate. At a minimum, however, our discussion provides useful suggestions of ways in which some of our conclusions might be in error and aids us in assessing the degree of confidence with which we should view our conclusions. The discussion also illustrates more general points. If we know or can reasonably assume the direction of bias present in data, then we can also assess the direction in which our conclusions are likely to be in error. If we also know or can reasonably assume the magnitude of bias present in data, we can assess the margin by which our conclusions are likely to be in error and even correct our estimates and arrive at more accurate conclusions. We will recall, of course, that random error has different effects and is not subject to the same partial remedies as is sometimes possible where bias is at issue.

Problems of Measurement and Comparison

Because of interest and curiosity, and to better understand long-term trends and patterns of change in the history and development of the United States, we would like to know more about the ways in which the diets of textile workers and their families compared with the diets of people today. To do so we need to compare, as we frequently must, things that are not fully comparable. Although we can rarely achieve precise comparability, we can follow lines of thought similar to those sketched above. By doing so we can sometimes assess the ways and even the degree in which conclusions based upon comparisons of the not fully comparable are likely to be in error. Such assessments allow us to draw more accurate conclusions or, at a minimum, suggest the need to qualify our conclusions in appropriate ways.

For purposes of comparison, table 7.5 gives (in the first column) estimates of per capita consumption of various food commodities by the population of the United States in 1985. [Table 7.5 is adapted from tables 179 and 180 (pp. 109–110) of the *Statistical Abstract of the United States, 1987* (Washington, D.C.: Government Printing Office, 1985).] Here again, it will be recognized that the values in the first column of the table are, in effect, averages. It is highly unlikely that any individual in 1985 had a diet exactly resembling that reflected in the table.

It will be recognized, of course, that the 1985 data given in the table are by no means fully comparable with those given in table 7.3. The food categories are not consistently the same; the units of measurement sometimes differ; and table 7.3 gives estimated food consumption per weighted family member. The 1985 data are simple per capita food consumption: estimated total consumption of the various food commodities divided by the total population of the United States. The question is, can we overcome these and other elements of incomparability and at least make useful comparisons? In making such comparisons can we also estimate the directions in which they are likely to be in error?

Greater comparability can be achieved. We can recalculate food consumption among the textile workers and their families on a simple per capita basis rather than in the weighted form used in table 7.3. For this purpose, the second column of table 7.5 gives simple per capita food consumption among the families calculated by summing the total amounts of each food commodity estimated as consumed by all families and dividing that total by the total number of individuals included in the families. It will be clear that combining, through summing, categories of 1985 consumption could be carried out to estimate consumption of the combined category. To do so, however, would not be entirely reliable as a means to assess consumption of the combined category.

Other incomparabilities can also be reduced. If we apply the old rule "a pint's a pound the world around," consumption estimates given in quarts and gallons can be converted to estimates of pounds consumed (or the reverse). At the end of the nineteenth century, a standard loaf of bread was conventionally treated as weighing one pound. In practice, bakers varied the weight of bread in relation to fluctuations in the cost of ingredients.

Table 7.5
Estimated Per Capita Consumption of Selected Food Commodities:
United States, 1985 and Textile Workers' Families, 1888-1890[a]

	1985	Textile Workers[b]
Beef	79.2	27.2
Veal	1.8	----
Lamb and Mutton	1.4	----
Meat(unspecified)	8.8	63.0
Pork (excluding lard)	62.0	23.9
Fish	14.5	7.0
Eggs (numbers)	255.0	125.8
Chicken	58.0	0.7 (poultry)
Turkey	12.1	----
Milk (quarts) [c]	247.3	57.1
Cheese	22.4	1.6
Butter	4.9	20.9
Margarine	10.8	----
Lard	1.8	15.6
Shortening	22.8	----
Other Edible Fats and Oils	21.3	----
Fruits [d]	149.3	----
Vegetables (except potatoes) [e]	125.3	----
Potatoes [e]	75.9	115.0
Sweet Potatoes [e]	4.6	----
Dry Edible Beans and Peas [e]	6.5	----
Sugar [f]	80.4	44.3
Corn Sweeteners	87.5	----
Molasses (gallons)	----	0.8
Flour, Meal and Cereals	168.4	238.5
Bread (loaves)	----	26.7
Rice	9.3	1.3
Coffee	10.0	6.9
Tea	----	2.6
Cocoa Beans	4.5	----

a All amounts in pounds unless otherwise indicated
b Families with income from boarders are excluded
c Includes milk, cream and specialties (such as sour cream, dips and eggnog) in 1985
d Includes fruit juices in 1985
e Data for 1984
f Includes non-caloric sweeteners in 1985

Even so, the convention of the time allows us to estimate the approximate number of pounds of bread consumed.

When we carry out adjustments and manipulations of this sort, two differences between estimated 1985 per capita food consumption and that of textile workers and their families are particularly striking. For one thing, the table suggests that diets tended to be much more varied in 1985 than among the families of textile workers. Secondly, the average quantity of food consumed per person in 1985 appears noticeably larger than in the earlier period. Should we take these differences as accurate; should we take them as products of error and incomparabilities; or should we take them as accurate but in need of qualification? To put the latter question differently, is it likely that actual differences were greater or smaller than those that appear in the table?

It is, of course, plausible to believe that more varied foods could be purchased in 1985 than at the end of the 1880s. It is also plausible that improvement of general economic conditions has meant that more people could enjoy a more varied, and more costly, diet by the 1980s than a century earlier. On the other hand, we should recall that in terms of income, the textile workers were probably below the average of the time. The data for 1985, in contrast, reflect the entire population of the United States. The appearance of greater variety is also produced in part by the use of more specific commodity categories in 1985 than for the earlier period. The question becomes, given these considerations, how must we qualify comparisons on the basis of data from table 7.5?

We confront similar problems in comparing quantities of food consumed. On first examination of table 7.5, the differences appear both striking and consistent. Average consumption of virtually all food commodities appears larger in 1985 than in the earlier years. The only exceptions are butter, lard, and flour as well as meal, bread, and other cereals; even the first two of these are probably spurious. When we sum estimated consumption of butter and lard for the earlier period the result is approximately 36 pounds per person. The sum of estimated consumption of all fats and oils (butter, margarine, lard, shortening, and other fats and oils) for 1985 is roughly 62 pounds per person. Moreover, not only do the quantities of food consumed appear larger in 1985, but also such high protein sources as meats, fish, eggs, and poultry, appear as larger components of diets than they did at the end of the 1880s. Once again, however, the question is how must we qualify our comparisons?

We can extend the comparisons begun in table 7.5 to examine the ways in which specific groups of textile workers compared with each other and with families today. To this end, table 7.6A gives the estimated total amounts of each food commodity consumed by each of the eight regional and nation-

Table 7.6a
Aggregate Amounts of Food Commodities Purchased, by Regional and Nationality Groups

	All Families	Northern Native - Stock	Northern French Canadian	Northern Canadian	Northern British	Northern Irish	Northern Continental European	Border Stae Native - Stock	Southern Native Stock
Beef	295,807	60,269	8,196	18,996	59,349	69,446	40,177	12,528	23,398
Pork	273,299	23,019	1,909	15,824	13,612	22,287	18,610	47,738	108,095
Meat	737,750	247,540	89,665	14,256	128,812	115,776	39,791	32,982	64,076
Fish	68,772	25,420	6,517	3,518	11,033	13,471	3,942	868	3,764
Eggs (doz)	113,291	25,854	16,075	6,622	21,325	19,199	8,754	5,107	9,598
Poultry	6,069	767	0	0	322	397	98	384	4,004
Milk	604,389	191,961	57,054	25,052	113,161	122,329	58,936	16,456	17,242
Cheese	18,478	3,130	1,717	869	4,785	3,167	1,570	440	2,638
Butter	227,702	59,482	17,887	10,105	43,753	45,893	19,647	15,014	14,097
Lard	164,962	36,758	13,182	6,419	18,444	17,307	11,361	16,710	42,941
Potatoes (bu.)	25,451	6,427	2,553	1,013	4,265	5,029	2,345	1,797	1,834
Sugar	479,391	134,127	35,746	16,453	83,993	90,132	34,736	32,529	47,748
Molasses (lbs.)	9,404	2,205	1,011	216	794	826	419	1,058	2,715
Flour and Meal	2,794,105	547,393	133,021	52,657	364,413	417,540	156,614	278,567	809,398
Bread (loaves)	311,757	44,791	99,309	45,760	34,126	40,663	35,300	3,130	4,880
Rice	13,900	522	1,199	304	1,243	430	1,016	386	8,388
Coffee	72,472	15,161	1,971	858	7,054	7,406	6,894	9,932	21,837
Tea	31,110	9,594	3,006	1,266	6,751	7,728	1,795	519	317

Table 7.6b
Number of Families and Individuals in Families, and Per Capita Food
by Regional and Nationality Groups

	All Families	Northern Native-Stock	Northern French Canadian	Northern Canadian	Northern British	Northern Irish	Northern Continental European	Border State Native-Stock	Southern Native Stock
Total Number of Individuals in Families	11,715	2,848	1,005	436	1,723	1,806	888	810	2,087
Beef									
Pork									
Meat									
Fish									
Eggs (doz)									
Poultry									
Milk									
Cheese									
Butter									
Lard									
Potatoes (bu.)									
Sugar									
Molasses (lbs.)									
Flour and Meal									
Bread (loaves)									
Rice									
Coffee									
Tea									

ality groups examined in earlier chapters. Chapter 7.6B gives the total number of individuals included in each of the eight groups. By using that information and the information in table 7.6A, simple per capita food consumption can be calculated for each group and food commodity and entered in table 7.6B. We can address the comparative quality of the diets of each group. We could also carry the comparisons a step farther by combining food categories to make comparisons with diets in our own times.

We can, of course, make these comparisons in any one of a number of different ways. Obviously, the most desirable approach would be to carry out the calculations and complete table 7.6B in its entirety. Alternatively, we might select two or more groups and limit our comparisons to just those groups. We might also select particular commodities and compare groups in terms of those commodities. Before carrying out the calculations, hypotheses should be formulated concerning the ways in which the quality of diets varied from one group to the other. Thought should also be given to the justification for the particular approach employed. If the groups are compared in terms of consumption of particular commodities, the justification for selecting these commodities rather than others should be considered.

By now readers will be concerned about the casual way we have shifted from the family weighted measure of per capita food consumption used in table 7.3 and 7.4 to the simple per capita measure employed in tables 7.5 and 7.6A and B and wonder whether the use of different measures in this fashion is likely to produce misinterpretations and unfounded conclusions. In fact the matter requires a good bit of thought.

In dealing with family income, three separate measures have been used: gross family income, per capita family income, and family weighted per capita income. In the case of food consumption, two different measures have been used: the family weighted measure in tables 7.3 and 7.4 and the simple per capita measure in tables 7.5 and table 7.6A and B. Of course, we also could have considered the total amounts spent by the families for the various food commodities. And table 7.6A gives the estimated gross amounts of each commodity that were consumed by each family.

It is obvious that each of these measures is deliberately biasing our data in different ways in order to take into account differences in the characteristics of the families. With a little thought we see that groups that tended to have larger families will appear relatively better off in comparison to groups with smaller families if measures of gross income or food consumption are used. In contrast, groups with smaller families will appear relatively better off when either of the per capita measures are used. When we use simple per capita income, differences in family size are taken into account, but groups with larger numbers of older children will compare more favorably with groups with more younger children than if the family weighted measure is employed. The latter measure is intended to take into account differences in the age and sex of family members as well as in the number of people in families.

We can recognize that still other measures of income or food consumption in relation to family size and composition could be employed. It might be argued, for example, that both of our per capita measures leave something out and rest, as a consequence, upon a faulty assumption. Both measures assume that burdens on income and family food supplies and other family requirements are directly proportional to the absolute size (the simple per capita measure) or the weighted size (the family weighted measure) of families.

We might argue that this approach neglects the "economies of scale" realized by larger families. Where food is concerned, the argument runs, these economies come in the form of purchasing in larger quantities at lower unit costs, less food waste in proportion to food costs, and less expensive dishes such as stews and soups that can be more cheaply prepared in larger than in smaller quantities. In this argument, it does not cost twice as much to feed a family of four as a family of two. Rent and fuel for a house of six rooms does not cost twice as much as for a house of three rooms, and these presumed economies need to be taken into account in designing and employing indexes to compare income and living conditions.

One approach that we might use for this purpose is to add a constant (two is often used) to family size (either absolute or weighted) in order to reflect these presumed economies. The consequences of such a "household weighted" measure will be readily apparent. With this measure, the food and other requirements and the demands upon income of a family of two would be increased by 100 percent (two family members plus the constant two), those of a family of four by 50 percent (four plus the constant two), and those of a family of six by one third in order to take into account assumed economies of scale. Using this approach, the requirements and burdens upon income presented by family members are increased by greater proportions for smaller than for larger families. (The implications of this approach can be examined by returning to the three families discussed in chapter 1.)

If we used this approach, regional and nationality groups—or, for that matter, income groups—characterized by larger families would tend to appear better off in comparison to groups with smaller families than when either the simple or the family weighted per capita measures are employed. It will be recognized that the "household weighted" measure involves very different assumptions about family life than the other two per capita measures. As a consequence, the amounts consumed by the families would appear quite different using the household measure and applying the assumptions it reflects.

Note that additional indexes could be devised, and that one index might be most appropriate for one aspect of family life, such as housing, while another might be most appropriate for another aspect, such as clothing or food. To better understand the consequences of the different measures and assumptions, it would be useful to return to the specific families considered in chapter 1 and recalculate their income levels using the three per capita income measures, noting the ways in which the comparisons of the families change when one measure is used as opposed to another. Tables 7.3 and 7.6 should also be reevaluated keeping in mind the differences in family characteristics between income and regional and nationality groups observed in earlier chapters. How would our conclusions concerning the comparative well being of the several groups differ if we used one per capita index rather than another?

A further question will also come to mind: Are these and other indexes most useful as means to describe the living conditions of families, are they most useful as means to compare the living conditions and relative well being of different groups of families, or both?

An even more central point should also be kept in mind. The results of comparing different groups in terms of income, food consumption, and other aspects of living conditions will depend upon the assumptions we make concerning family characteristics, processes, and practices. Differences will result, as well, from the differing assumptions we make concerning the error characteristic of our original data.

We must recognize, moreover, that assumptions cannot be avoided. A little thought about the data for 1985 given in table 7.5 will demonstrate that the need for assumptions is not confined to historical inquiry and is in fact a necessary element of thinking and understanding. The questions concern only the justifications for the particular assumptions employed, their plausibility, and our views and theories concerning family processes and practices. We can similarly recognize that these considerations can be used to provide tests of observed differences and relationships. When differences are observed between groups, we should ask whether any plausible assumptions could be made that would eliminate, reduce, or reverse these differences. A further point also follows: assumptions should be recognized and made explicit rather than ignored or concealed. They should be subjected to critical evaluation rather than thoughtlessly accepted at face value.

PROBLEMS OF OMISSION
AND MISINTERPRETATION

When one neglects factors that are relevant to the process or phenomena of concern, erroneous conclusions and misleading comparisons result. Errors of omission occur in many ways. One example is provided by chapter 6, where we were unable to adequately measure home production of clothing so that, as we noted, the quality of family dress was underestimated. Examination of the descriptive comments of interviewers given in the sample page in our Introduction will suggest a further omission that is clearly relevant here: The interviewers' comments indicate that, as in the case of clothing, some families had supplementary sources of food that are not reflected in the amounts of specific commodities given in the source collection as purchased or consumed or in our estimates of food consumption given in table 7.6 and related tables.

The interviewers' comments give us limited means to address these problems of omission and underestimation. The comments do not, of course, allow us to estimate the specific amounts of commodities that were available to families over and above the amounts that they reported purchasing. We can use the comments, however, to gain limited information to assess the ways and degrees to which our conclusions and interpretations are likely to be biased if we overlook the supplementary food sources available to the families.

For these purposes we would like to use the interviewers' comments to address limited questions of the following sort. How many families had supplementary food sources and of what kinds? Do tables 7.3, 7.5 and 7.6 tend to systematically underestimate consumption of particular foodstuffs and if so which foods? If supplementary food sources are taken into account, do particular groups of families appear better (or worse) off than they appear in tables 7.3 and 7.6? Did disproportionate numbers of lower income families have supplementary food sources, so that, for example, their standard of living actually compared more favorably with higher income families than table 7.3 suggests, or was it instead the higher income families that tended to have supplementary sources? Were particular regional and nationality groups better or worse off in comparison to other groups than table 7.6 tends to indicate?

To address some of these questions, table 7.7 tabulates the supplementary food sources available to families, as indicated by the interviewers' comments, in several different ways. Panel A of the table gives for each of the eight regional and nationality groups categorized by per capita income quartile, the percentage of families that had at least one supplementary food source, no supplementary food sources, and the percentage for whom no interviewers' comment is available. Note that some families had more than one supplementary food source. Panel B of the table gives the percentage of families with different types of food sources. Of the Northern native-stock families, for example, 10 percent had gardens. Note again, that some families had more than one supplementary source. Panel C gives the percentage

Table 7.7A
Percentage of Families With Supplementary Food Sources by
Per Capita Income Quartile and Regional and Nationality Group [1]

| | Number of Suppl. Food Sources | Per Capita Income Quartile | | | | |
		First Quartile	Second Quartile	Third Quartile	Fourth Quartile	Total
Northern Native - Stock Families	One or More	11%	16%	10%	14%	13%
	None	79%	75%	81%	70%	76%
	Unknown [2]	10%	9%	9%	16%	11%
	Total	100%	100%	100%	100%	100%
Northern French Canadian Families	One or More	0%	0%	2%	0%	1%
	None	92%	95%	93%	86%	92%
	Unknown [2]	8%	5%	5%	14%	7%
	Total	100%	100%	100%	100%	100%
Northern Canadian-Stock Families	One or More	4%	7%	0%	13%	6%
	None	57%	80%	85%	60%	67%
	Unknown [2]	39%	13%	15%	27%	27%
	Total	100%	100%	100%	100%	100%
Northern British- Stock Families	One or More	9%	11%	14%	20%	15%
	None	89%	79%	83%	71%	78%
	Unknown [2]	2%	10%	3%	9%	7%
	Total	100%	100%	100%	100%	100%
Northern Irish- Stock Families	One or More	8%	11%	7%	13%	11%
	None	80%	72%	84%	71%	76%
	Unknown [2]	12%	16%	9%	16%	13%
	Total	100%	100%	100%	100%	100%
Northern Continental European-Stock Families	One or More	20%	9%	11%	16%	14%
	None	65%	82%	78%	63%	72%
	Unknown [2]	15%	9%	11%	21%	14%
	Total	100%	100%	100%	100%	100%
Border State Native - Stock Families	One or More	34%	39%	46%	22%	36%
	None	62%	56%	51%	74%	60%
	Unknown [2]	4%	5%	3%	4%	4%
	Total	100%	100%	100%	100%	100%
Southern Native- Stock Families	One or More	33%	42%	35%	25%	34%
	None	65%	55%	62%	74%	64%
	Unknown [2]	2%	3%	3%	1%	2%
	Total	100%	100%	100%	100%	100%

1 Families with paying boarders are excluded from all categories in this table.

2 The "Unknown" category contains families for which no interviewer comments were provided.

of families in the eight regional and nationality groups with given numbers of food sources. Of the Northern native-stock families, for example, four percent had two supplementary food sources while 11 percent of the Southern native stock had two sources.

Our task is to use table 7.7 to address questions of the sort posed above and to modify and qualify generalizations based upon tables 7.3 through 7.6. It will be clear that each of the panels in table 7.7 addresses the data in somewhat different ways, and each is, therefore, relevant to some questions and generalizations but not to others. Care should be exercised to avoid using the wrong tabulation in addressing particular questions. A major source of erroneous conclusions is to employ data and tabulations to support conclusions that the tabulations really do not address.

Table 7.7B
Percentage of Families With Various Types of Supplementary
Food Sources by Regional and Nationality Group [1]

Type of Supplementary Food Source

	None	Gardens	Farms	Poultry	Pigs	Cows	Fruits	Unknown	Total
Northern Native-Stock Families	73%	10%	1%	5%	0%	1%	0%	11%	100%
Northern French Canadian Families	92%	0%	1%	0%	0%	0%	0%	7%	100%
Northern Canadian Families	67%	3%	3%	0%	0%	0%	0%	27%	100%
Northern British Families	77%	12%	0%	3%	0%	0%	2%	6%	100%
Northern Irish Families	74%	7%	0%	2%	0%	2%	2%	13%	100%
Northern Continental European Families	68%	14%	0%	5%	0%	0%	0%	13%	100%
Border State Native-Stock Families	49%	18%	2%	18%	1%	8%	1%	3%	100%
Southern Native-Stock Families [2]	54%	16%	1%	14%	4%	9%	0%	2%	100%

1 The few families reporting more than one supplementary food source are included under each food source contained in the table, thus slightly increasing the base of families upon which these kpercentages were calculated.

2 One family reported that they kept bees.

Before concluding this chapter we must clearly recognize a further and central point. Problems of omission of the sort encountered here are by no means confronted only in the case of our source collection nor are they confined to historical inquiry. A consistent problem confronted in all studies of economic productivity, living conditions, and social and economic well being is inability to adequately assess the additional production provided by the work of wives in the home and in caring for children, the "do it yourself" work and home maintenance of husbands and other family members and, as in the present case, home food and clothing production. And these are only a few examples of the kinds of unaccounted productivity that is at best imperfectly measured in social and economic studies whether historical or contemporary in their orientations.

Our problem is always to recognize the existence of such omissions and attempt to assess their impact upon our comparisons, findings and conclusions. Here a final question is in order. In what ways, if at all, are the supplementary food sources of textile workers likely to affect the compari-

Table 7.7c
Percentage of Families With Specified Number of Supplementary
Food Sources Available by Regional and Nationality Group

	Number of Food Sources Available					
	None	One	Two	Three or More	Unknown	Total
Northern Native-Stock Families	76%	10%	3%	0%	11%	100%
Northern French Canadian Families	92%	1%	0%	0%	7%	100%
Northern Canadian Families	67%	6%	0%	0%	27%	100%
Northern British Families	78%	12%	3%	0%	7%	100%
Northern Irish Families	76%	8%	2%	1%	13%	100%
Northern Continental European Families	72%	9%	4%	1%	14%	100%
Border State Native-Stock Families	60%	18%	15%	3%	4%	100%
Southern Native-Stock Families [2]	64%	19%	11%	4%	2%	100%

sons given in table 7.5? Is it likely that people today have greater or lesser access to supplementary food sources than families at the end of the 1880s?

— 8 —
THE LIVING CONDITIONS
OF INDUSTRIAL WORKERS

This chapter addresses two primary problems. One involves the sources of differences in family living conditions. In preceding chapters we have observed rather striking and systematic differences in living conditions between particular groups of families. Now we would like to learn more about the causes of those differences. Although as we proceed we will need to use a little care in our use of the word "cause," our examination yields additional information concerning the structure of the economy and society at the end of the century.

Our second problem concerns the generalizability of our findings. We have subjected our group of over 3,000 textile workers and their families to intensive examination, and we have learned a great deal about their characteristics, their practices, their way of life, and even something of their preferences. We must now assess the strengths and limitations of our findings. We know that this group of families is not a probability sample in the contemporary sense of the word. Are our findings, then, limited in their relevance to just this specific group of families? Can we draw inferences about other and larger groups of families and individuals and, if so, what groups of families and individuals? Put differently, our question is what have we really learned about life at the end of the nineteenth century?

VARIATIONS IN EARNINGS

From the preceding chapters and with common sense, we can easily specify a number of the factors that shaped the living conditions of these and other families and produced differences among them. Difference in income was surely one of these factors; all things being equal, a higher income generally will result in a better standard of living. Family size—variations in the burdens on family income produced by differences in the number of family members—was a further determining factor. At the same levels of income, smaller families generally tended to have better living conditions than larger families. Here it will be clear, of course, that we refer only to material standards of living. Although less readily measurable, regional and local variations in prices and the availability of commodities and services also affected living conditions as did such even less easily measured factors as housekeeping practices and the extent of home production.

We also know, however, that these were wage earning families. Their primary source of income was the wages of family members. The earnings of husbands constituted, on the average, by far the largest component of family income and were therefore a primary source of differences in family living conditions. It is likely, moreover, that the same factors that influenced the wages and earnings of husbands also influenced the wages and earnings of other family members. Examination of sources of variation in the earnings of husbands is of both intrinsic interest and can also move us toward better understanding of why living conditions differed from one family or group of families to the next.

EARNINGS AND NATIONALITY

Here again, we already know some of the factors that influenced the earnings of textile workers. Wages and earnings varied from one region of the nation to the other. Earnings were clearly lower in the South and the Border States than in the North. It is virtually certain that local variations in wages and earnings existed within these larger regions. Wages and earnings undoubtedly varied with skill and experience and from one occupation to the next. Occupations that required higher levels of skills or involved greater supervisory authority or other responsibilities commanded higher wages than other occupations.

These and related issues are addressed in the discussion that follows. In this discussion, however, we are primarily concerned with the effects of differences in national background upon wages and earnings. Our basic hypothesis is that foreign-stock groups—or at least some foreign-stock groups—tended to have lower earnings because of their foreign backgrounds. The explanatory formulation runs roughly along the following lines: Foreign-stock workers, or particular groups of them, tended to have lower earnings because of certain of their characteristics—educational, cultural, linguistic, or the like—or because of the adverse attitudes and reactions to them on the part of other population groups. As a result, foreign-stock workers tended to receive lower wages, had greater difficulty finding employment, experienced layoffs more frequently, and were at a disadvantage in competing for better jobs. As is sometimes said of black workers in our own day, they were the last hired and the first fired and this situation was reflected in their poorer living conditions.

This is certainly a plausible hypothesis. Numerous historical studies and contemporary accounts detail the plight of the foreign stock and describe the difficulties that they faced in the New World. In the present case, however, the hypothesis is by no means completely open and shut. Many of these historical studies and accounts focus upon the "newer" immigrants from eastern and southern Europe who entered the United States in great numbers at the end of the nineteenth century and during the earlier decades of the twentieth. It was particularly these groups that were marked by language and educational liabilities, by cultural characteristics that sometimes worked to their disadvantage, and who experienced discrimination at the hands of native- and other foreign-stock groups.

In contrast, the foreign-stock textile workers reflected in the present source collection were not the products of this "new" immigration. Rather, they were with few exceptions of western and northern European or Canadian backgrounds. They were probably often less sharply differentiated from the native stock in cultural, linguistic, and educational terms. It is likely that as part of an older immigration, processes of acculturation had worked for some groups to further diminish whatever differences and disadvantages they brought with them to the United States from their former homelands. It is not necessarily the case that all of the groups reflected in the source collection suffered the same disadvantages in comparison to the native stock.

The hypothesis is also not entirely open and shut on other grounds. We cannot address the hypothesis directly. For one thing, our source collection tells us nothing of the educational levels, linguistic competence, or related characteristics of the textile workers nor does it provide information on the attitudes of particular native- and foreign-stock groups toward each other.

The second and more general reason is that causal formulations Such as this one cannot be tested directly. To explore the hypothesis, therefore, we can only resort to a more circuitous and in some ways less satisfying route that involves ruling out alternative explanations of differences in earnings between the various groups. That route will serve only to increase or decrease our confidence in the validity of the hypothesis; it will lead neither to definitive support nor to refutation. In pursuing that route, however, we gain additional information bearing upon the situation of foreign- and native-stock groups at the end of the century.

ALTERNATIVE EXPLANATIONS

We must first establish that differences in earnings between native- and foreign-stock groups actually existed. As will be recalled, our work in chapter 2 indicated that in the Northern states, foreign-stock textile workers, taken as a single group, did tend to have lower earnings than native-stock workers. As will also be recalled, this finding was limited to the North because the very small number of foreign-stock workers in the Southern and Border States precluded meaningful comparison. For the same reason, our examination here must be limited to the North.

When more specific groups of foreign-stock workers were examined in chapter 2, we found, however, that the earnings of workers of some nationalities compared favorably with or even exceeded those of the native stock. It is superficially easy to take a further step in establishing these differences by comparing the median yearly earnings of Northern husbands and of husbands in each of the six specific nationality groups considered in earlier chapters. When that is done, we find that the median annual earnings of the Northern groups appear as $485 for the native stock, $453 for the British, $383 for the Continental Europeans, and $367, $358, and $345 respectively for the Irish, French Canadians and Canadians. For purposes of comparison, the median annual earnings of the Border State and Southern native-stock husbands are $343 and $250.

These differences may seem quite small; indeed, our first reaction might be to consider them insignificant. Certainly the differences in earnings between some groups is smaller than in the case of others. One way to interpret these differences and to assess their significance is in terms of the prices and expenditures given in chapters 6 and 7. On the basis of table 7.2 it can be noted, for example, that $32, the approximate difference between the median annual earnings of Northern native-stock and British husbands, would buy nearly 200 pounds of beef at average New England prices.

It does appear, as was expected, that the annual earnings of Northern native-stock textile workers did tend to be higher than those of workers of other nationalities. The annual earnings of the Continental European husbands, the Irish, and the two groups of Canadians amount to only about three-fourths of those of the native stock. Only the earnings of British husbands compare favorably with those of the native stock. A closer look at the range and distribution around the medians of the earnings of husbands would show that some foreign-stock husbands did have higher earnings than the native stock. Even so, the earnings of the foreign stock appear lower on the average than the native stock. A second conclusion might be that these differences were the consequences of intrinsic characteristics of the foreign stock, or of the attitudes of other groups toward them, that placed the foreign stock at a disadvantage.

Before we accept these conclusions, reservations must be entertained on at least two grounds. For one thing, our analytic methods are crude and subject to distortion. We might ponder, for example, whether simple examination of medians is a satisfactory means by which to identify differences between the several groups. But however convincing the examination of the data may or may not be, it will be clear that the second conclusion is subject to a possible fallacy. It is certainly possible, in fact probable, that other factors in addition to differences in national background contributed to differences in earnings. It is possible, indeed, that differences in earnings were due entirely to other factors and had nothing to do with the intrinsic characteristics of the foreign stock or with the attitudes of other groups toward them. In other words, the apparent causal relationship between national background and difference in earnings may be spurious.

We will immediately think of a number of factors, some of them more far-fetched than others, that might account for the relationship between national background and earnings. At least three such possibilities can be tested on the basis of the data collection. One of these has to do with age. If native-stock textile workers tended to be older than foreign-stock workers, we might suspect that differences in earnings were due in part to the greater experience and seniority of the former group and not to differences in national background. A second possibility is that the foreign stock were disproportionately clustered in low income areas of the nation. If so, we might argue that the lower earnings of the foreign stock were due to the accident of place of residence and not to the intrinsic characteristics of the groups in question. A third possibility is that the foreign stock were disproportionately clustered in occupations of lower skill and responsibility and that differences in earnings were due largely to occupational differences. Such a finding would not, of course, necessarily suggest that the foreign stock were without disadvantages in comparison to the native stock.

As will be recalled, the ages of foreign- and native-stock husbands were compared in passing in chapter 4. We found that in the North, the native stock tended to be younger than the foreign stock. Thus the possibility that differences in earnings were really due to the greater skill, experience, and seniority gained through the years by older native-stock workers seems to be weakened. It is worth pondering whether the comparisons in chapter 4 really provide sufficient grounds for dismissing such possibilities entirely. Consideration of this issue can be deferred for the moment. The other two possibilities require more detailed examination.

It is certainly possible that annual earnings varied not only between the Southern and Border states, on the one hand, and the North, on the other, but also within these regions. We can readily imagine that the wage structure, employment opportunities, and unemployment rates varied from one subregion to the other, from state to state, and for that matter from locality to locality within states. A hint of that variation is provided by comparison of annual earnings in the New England states represented in the data collection (Connecticut, Maine, Massachusetts, New Hampshire, and Rhode Island) with the Middle Atlantic States (Delaware, New Jersey, New York, and Pennsylvania). In the former group of states, median annual earnings for all husbands in the families of textile workers appear as approximately $413 as compared to $453 in the latter states, a difference of some $40 per year. Comparison on a state-by-state basis indicates in some instances even larger differences.

Our question is whether differences in earnings between the native and foreign stock, or particular foreign-stock groups, can be accounted for in terms of differences in area of residence and employment. To explore this possibility table 8.1 compares the various national groups in the North in terms of median annual earnings. We again use the same six nationality categories that were employed in earlier chapters, and these are in turn subdivided in relation to region of residence. In other words, the table compares the annual earnings of the several groups holding region of residence constant.

As we can see, the table does not provide consistent support for the possibility that the relationship between earnings and background observed above was actually the product of place residence and employment. It does appear that New England tended to be a lower wage area than the Middle Atlantic states, although the differences are ambiguous. Within each of the regions, however, the annual earnings of native-stock husbands, followed by the British, appear higher than those of other groups. Thus the higher earnings of native-stock and British workers persists even when region of residence and employment is controlled and held constant. The two groups of Canadian workers were concentrated in the New England states. It is possible, therefore, that the earnings of these groups were depressed due to their residence in a lower-paying area. However, we cannot take differences in earnings between the several nationality groups as nothing more than the product of differences in area of residence and employment.

The third possibility sketched above concerns occupation. The question is whether foreign-stock workers, or particular groups thereof, were disproportionately clustered in lower skilled, less responsible, and hence, lower paid occupations while the native stock and, perhaps, particular groups of the foreign stock tended to monopolize higher paying occupations.

The husbands are given in the data collection as employed in some 158 specific occupations, including the categories "idle" and "invalid." The names of a number of these specific occupations—watchman, janitor, foreman, overseer are examples—are identifiable; and we have at least intuitive notions of the degree of skill, responsibility, or supervisory duties that they involved. The majority are less meaningful. The relative skill or responsibility required, for example, of a "beamer and twister" as compared with a "gigger," "gigger's helper," or "spinner-mule" is by no means obvious.

Fortunately, the Department of Labor published in 1918 a brief volume entitled *Description of Occupations: Textiles and Clothing*[1] prepared by the Bureau of Labor Statistics. This volume provides systematic information bearing upon the qualifications, duties, and related occupations for over 500 specific occupations in textile and clothing manufacturing. Of the 158 specific occupations included in the data collection, approximately 90 percent are listed in this volume.

Using this source of information, we can group the specific occupations included in the data collection into five more general categories in order of skill and responsibility. The categories are (1) supervisors, (2) foremen and second hands, (3) skilled laborers and craftsmen, (4) semi-skilled laborers,

Table 8.1
Median Annual Earnings and Number of Husbands
by Nationality Group and Region

	Native Stock	British	Continental Europe	Irish	French Canada	Canada	Median
New England:							
Earnings	$466	$434	$359	$377	$358	$345	$414
Number of Husbands	(351)	(215)	(120)	(238)	(223)	(92)	
Middle Atlantic:							
Earnings	$499	$480	$421	$349	NA*	NA*	$453
Number of Husbands	(398)	(228)	(101)	(226)	(3)	(4)	
All North:							
Earnings	$485	$452	$382	$366	$358	$345	$429
Number of Husbands	(749)	(443)	(221)	(464)	(226)	(96)	

*Number of cases too small for generalization.

and (5) common laborers. Residual categories composed of the small number of white collar workers, occupations that could not be identified, and individuals for whom no occupation is given are excluded from our tabulations.

We can recognize that this categorization scheme is inevitably imperfect. The descriptions of the various specific occupations are sometimes ambiguous. In using the Department of Labor volume, we assume that occupations in the textile industry were roughly the same at the end of the 1880s as they were some thirty years later. The fact that most of the occupations given in the data collection are also listed in the Department of Labor volume may increase our confidence in this assumption.

A partial means to assess the adequacy of this categorization of occupations is by examining its relation to earnings. In general it would be expected that the greater the skill and responsibility required by a given occupation, the higher the wages and the greater the earnings would be. In fact, a relationship is present. The correlation between occupation and earnings is moderately strong ($r = -.54$). (This negative relationship reflects our inverse ranking of the occupational categories from the most skilled and responsible to the least skilled and responsible.) The relationship, however, is not perfect, a point that is further suggested by examination of table 8.2. Median annual earnings do increase from the lowest skill category through the more highly skilled categories to the supervisory categories. But the minimum and maximum values suggest considerable variation within and between categories. As we can see, for example, some common laborers (probably only a few) had higher annual earnings than the median earnings of supervisors.

It is useful to pause and briefly consider factors that explain the departures from perfect association between occupation and annual earnings. It is likely that some unknown number of occupations have been misclassified. Doubtlessly, if we could classify all specific occupations correctly, the association between earnings and occupation would appear stronger. The appearance of extreme values in table 8.2 is a further factor working to depress that association. The extremes of very high and very low annual earnings suggested by the table may reflect the presence of error in the data or a small number of unusual cases ("outliers"). By the same token, the appearance of zero values in the table (no annual earnings) can be taken as suggesting that at least some husbands, although they did have an occupation, were without work during the course of the year.

The latter issue suggests a more general point and an element of ambiguity. The earnings of husbands listed in the data collection are the total amounts reported as earned in the course of the year. In the immediate sense, annual earnings were affected by both wage levels and the number of days and hours actually worked. A supervisor would receive higher wages than a common laborer, but if he worked only a fraction of the year, his total annual earnings might be lower than those of a common laborer who worked for the full year.

While we must keep considerations such as these in mind, the classification scheme allows us to explore the possibility that foreign-stock groups were disproportionately employed in lower paying occupations with the consequence of lower earnings. Table 8.3 assesses this possibility by cross-tabulating the national backgrounds of husbands against their occupations for the New England states (Panel A) and for the Middle Atlantic region (Panel B).

Looking first at New England, we find that the higher paid occupations tended to be disproportionately held by native-stock workers while lower paid occupations were disproportionately the domains of workers of other nationalities. The native stock accounted for some 59 percent of all supervisors and almost 48 percent of the foremen. Only some 29 percent of the New England textile workers included in the data collection were of native stock. In other words, the native stock were overrepresented by some 30 percentage points among supervisors and almost 19 percentage points among foremen. Conversely, the native stock were underrepresented by some nine percentage points in each of the two lower skilled occupational categories.

The pattern for the other nationality groups appears relatively consistent: overrepresentation in the lower skilled categories and underrepresentation in the higher skilled and supervisory occupations. The British, however, tend to be somewhat better represented in the higher skilled and supervisory categories than other foreign-stock groups. The Canadians and French Canadians appear particularly overrepresented in the lower skilled (and lower paid) occupations.

We find somewhat the same pattern in the Middle Atlantic states (table

Table 8.2
Median, Minimum and Maximum Earnings of Husbands

	Median	Minimum	Maximum	Number
Supervisors	$768	$150	$1,937	152
Foreman	500	125	1,800	221
Skilled Laborers	465	0	1,500	961
Semi-Skilled Laborers	376	19	1,007	742
Common Laborers	306	0	1,456	652

8.3 Panel B). Here, however, the differences between the several nationality groups are less sharp, and the groups are represented in the various occupational categories more nearly in proportion to their total representation in the data collection. The native stock are overrepresented among foremen, underrepresented in the common labor category, and in the other three categories represented in approximate proportion to their representation in the data collection. The British are noticeably overrepresented among supervisors, underrepresented in the common labor category, and in the other three categories distributed more in accord with to their representation in the data collection. The overrepresentation of the Irish in the common labor category is noteworthy.

It appears, then, that the higher skilled and supervisory occupations were disproportionately filled by the native stock. In both the New England and Middle Atlantic States, the British occupied the next most favored position. In New England, the two groups of Canadians apparently competed least well for better paying and higher status employment. In the absence of Canadians in the Middle Atlantic states, workers of Irish and

Table 8.3
Nationality of Husbands Employed in Occupational Categories
by Regions (In Percentages)

New England

	Supervisors	Foreman	Skilled Laborers	Semi-Skilled Laborers	Common Laborers	Total
Native Stock	59.3%	47.7%	31.0%	20.9%	21.6%	29.0%
British	18.5%	13.5%	23.0%	19.1%	9.8%	18.0%
Cont. Europe	5.6%	9.0%	6.4%	15.8%	6.7%	9.3%
Irish	11.1%	8.1%	22.3%	13.4%	24.7%	18.5%
Fr. Canadians	1.9%	15.3%	12.9%	22.1%	29.0%	18.7%
Canadians	3.7%	6.3%	4.4%	8.7%	8.2%	6.6%
Total	100.1%	99.9%	100.0%	100.0%	100.0%	100.1%
Number	54	111	435	335	255	

Middle Atlantic

	Supervisors	Foreman	Skilled Laborers	Semi-Skilled Laborers	Common Laborers	Total
Native Stock	44.6%	58.7%	46.0%	48.4%	30.6%	43.8%
British	39.3%	19.6%	29.0%	23.6%	16.6%	24.8%
Irish	12.5%	15.2%	15.3%	13.8%	38.9%	20.0%
Cont. Europe	3.6%	6.5%	9.8%	14.2%	12.4%	11.1%
Total	100.0%	100.0%	100.1%	100.0%	100.1%	100.0%
Number	56	46	307	254	193	

Continental European backgrounds were least favored in terms of occupation.

We know, of course, that earnings varied from one worker to the next in the same occupational category. It is possible, therefore, that within occupational categories earnings varied in relation to national background. To explore this possibility table 8.4 gives the median annual earnings of each nationality group for each occupational category. Once again, New England is examined separately from the Middle Atlantic states. As indicated, the numbers of cases for some categories are quite small, and care must be exercised in interpreting the table.

The patterns, however, are quite clear and consistent. With three exceptions, the median earnings of native-stock workers were highest in each occupational category in both regions. In both regions British supervisors had higher median earnings than native-stock supervisors and the median earnings of British semi-skilled workers in New England appear slightly higher than the native stock. With a few exceptions the earnings of British workers are higher than those of other foreign-stock groups in both regions and each occupational category. Again with a few exceptions, the median earnings of the two New England Canadian groups are lowest in each occupational category. In the Middle Atlantic states, the earnings of the Irish appear lowest to the degree that the number of cases is large enough to allow comparison.

Native-stock and, to a lesser degree, British textile workers were more frequently employed in higher skilled and supervisory occupations than workers of other nationalities. But the fact of employment in higher paying occupations was only part of the story. Native-stock and British workers also tended to have higher earnings than workers of other nationalities employed in the same occupations. Canadians, Irish, and Continental Europeans were, it seems, at a twofold disadvantage. They were less successful in competing for higher paying jobs, but even when successful their earnings tended to be lower than those of native-stock or British workers in the same occupations.

These findings increase our confidence in the view that among the textile workers and their families, difference in earnings and, hence, in living conditions were related to nationality. The findings suggest that some foreign-stock groups were at a disadvantage in comparison to other groups and to the native stock. At a minimum we cannot write differences in earnings off as due to differences in region of residence and employment or occupation. Earnings differentials persist even when these factors are held constant. The earnings of some foreign-stock groups were quite consistently lower than other groups and than the native stock within the same region and occupational category.

FURTHER INFERENCES:
INDUSTRIAL WORKERS IN THE UNITED STATES

These are all interesting and potentially important findings. We have a reasonably comprehensive picture of these families; we know a good bit about differences in family size from one group to the next; we have a number of plausible inferences concerning differences in family practices along with a detailed view of aspects of their conditions of life, and extensive information concerning their levels and sources of income. We even have partial but highly plausible explanations of some of the factors that produced differences in income and living conditions.

But how far can we press these findings? We have assumed that this group of families provides a basis for conclusions about larger groups of families and individuals at the time, and that by examining these families we can gain more general knowledge of life in the United States at the end of the nineteenth century. We must now confront these assumptions directly. To what degree can we use this group of textile workers and their

Table 8.4
Median Earnings in Dollars of Occupational Categories by Nationality Group and Region

A. New England

	Supervisors	Foreman	Skilled Laborers	Semi-Skilled Laborers	Common Laborers
Native Stock	$800	$545	$492	$391	$374
British	875*	507*	466	397	365*
Cont. Europe	**	**	435	340	326
Irish	**	**	447	367	315
Fr. Canadians	**	438*	473	345	317
Canadians	**	**	466	329	291*

B. Middle Atlantic

	Supervisors	Foreman	Skilled Laborers	Semi-Skilled Laborers	Common Laborers
Native Stock	$775	$506	$546	$472	$399
British	837*	**	521	471	350
Irish	**	**	407	423	307
Cont. Europe	**	**	501	441	343

* Twenty-five or fewer cases.
** Ten or fewer cases.

families to draw valid and reliable inferences about other and larger groups of families and individuals? To address this question we must locate the group of families within the larger population of the time. Put differently, the question is how representative is this group of families and of what groups is it representative?

We can recognize that these questions pose major research tasks and, because of the characteristics of historical source material, tasks that could never be fully completed. We can, however, gain some clarification of the problem, and we can increase our confidence in the broader relevance of our findings by addressing several interrelated questions. First, what population groups do the data not represent? Second, what groups are the data most likely to represent? Third, how plausible are our findings and how consistent are they with findings based upon other sources? Finally, can inferences be drawn on the basis of this source collection that are likely to be applicable to larger groups almost regardless of the representative or nonrepresentative character of the collection?

We can address the first question quite briefly. Clearly, the collection does not represent the entire population of families, households, or individuals in the United States at the time. As examples, the sample does not include, deliberately, households composed of a single individual nor was it designed to be representative of business proprietors or medical doctors, lawyers, or other professionals. The collection was not intended to provide a basis for examining farmers or farm laborers and their families or members of the upper class. Other examples of groups that the sample does not represent will also come to mind. The collection was intended to be representative of textile workers and their families; it may be representative of industrial workers more generally, or, somewhat more dubiously, of the urban working class. It is likely, moreover, that we can draw some inferences that would be applicable to other groups of the time.

Questions of the plausibility of findings and the consistency of the data and findings with other information sources are more difficult to address. We can make a beginning, however, by reexamining some of the patterns and relationships observed in this and preceding chapters both to assess plausibility and in an effort to detect possible biases.

To make the point more forcefully, we can state these issues and questions in an alternative and more extreme form. Is it conceivable that officials of the office of the Commissioner of Labor somehow managed to select for interviewing native-stock families of textile workers who had substantially higher earnings and smaller families than most native-stock workers? Is it also conceivable that they selected foreign-stock workers with lower earnings and larger families than most of the foreign stock? In this extreme and implausible case, the higher earnings and superior living conditions of the native stock would be spurious, the reverse of actual fact, and a product of sample "bias" rather than a reflection of reality.

There is little reason to put much stock in this possibility. We know that the officials who conducted the survey attempted to select representative families and believed that they had done so, although they also admitted imperfections. On the basis of other evidence, we have little reason to doubt that outside the South and the Border States, native-stock workers tended to have higher earnings and to be more frequently employed in better and higher paid occupations. Contemporary accounts and secondary studies, based upon less systematic sources, document patterns similar to those reported above. When systematic data bearing upon workers and their families employed in coal mining and iron, steel, coke, and glass manufacturing are examined, much the same differences in occupation, earnings, and income appear. How much confidence to place in the precise magnitudes of differences between population groups or occupations is another matter.

We can say much the same of family size. Studies have been conducted that indicate that some foreign-stock population groups did tend to have larger numbers of children than the native stock or other specific nationality groups. Given the plausibility of differences in income and family size, differences in living conditions also become more plausible.

At first glance the greater number of foreign-stock than native-stock textile workers in most of the Northern states may strike us as implausible and as an indication of possible sample bias. Although numerous, people of foreign stock constituted a minority of the national population in these years. Most of the population was native-born of native-born parents. Is it plausible to find that some 72 percent of New England and 59 percent of Middle Atlantic textile workers were of foreign stock?

In fact this distribution is quite plausible. The concentration of foreign-stock population was greater in the Northern states represented in the data collection than in the United States as a whole. The Northern industrial labor force was composed disproportionately of foreign stock. We can gain partial but suggestive support for the point by drawing upon data collected through the 1890 Census of the United States and given in table 8.5. The table gives for the New England and Middle Atlantic states included in the data collection the percentage of foreign- and native-stock white workers employed in the "manufacturing and mechanical industries," the census employment category that includes the textile industry. (The percentages of black workers employed in this category in the North was very small.) Also given for each region and for the combined Northern states are the percentages of foreign- and native-stock textile workers included in the data collection.

As we can see the percentages of foreign- and native-stock textile workers do not depart greatly from the percentage of foreign and native stock included in the Census manufacturing and mechanical industries category. The foreign stock are more heavily represented among New England textile workers than among workers in the manufacturing and mechanical industries and the reverse appears in the case of the Middle Atlantic states. When summed to the entire North the percentage of foreign and native stock among textile workers is approximately the same as in the census manufacturing and mechanical industries category. We have, therefore, little reason to consider the larger percentage of foreign- than of native-stock workers included in the data collection as implausible or suggestive of a biased sample.

Because of the inadequacy of historical source material, the plausibility of the levels of earnings and income reflected in the data collection is more difficult to assess. Data bearing upon income and earnings in the latter nineteenth and earlier twentieth centuries are fragmentary, complex, and tend to be unsystematic. Even so, a number of scholars have drawn imaginatively and laboriously on the available sources to construct estimates of income and earnings for these years. We cannot carry out here anything approaching a thorough examination of these estimates. We can, however, draw upon two series of estimates for illustrative and suggestive information.

The first series is provided by Paul H. Douglas' pioneering work *Real Wages in the United States, 1890–1926.*[2] Drawing upon the United States

Table 8.5
National Background of Textile Workers and of White Workers Employed in the "Manufacturing and Mechanical Industries"

	Manufacturing and Mechanical Industries		Textile Workers	
	Foreign Stock	Native Stock	Foreign Stock	Native Stock
New England	63.1%	36.9%	71.7%	28.3%
Middle Atlantic	62.9	37.2	58.5	41.5
North	63.9	37.1	65.9	34.1

*Source: Department of the Interior, Census Office, *Report on the Population of the United States at the Eleventh Census, 1890,* (Government Printing Office: Washington, D. C. 1897).

Census and other sources, Douglas provides national estimates of average annual earnings of employed wage earners, salaried employees, and professionals in some thirty or more categories for the period in question. Examples are given in table 8.6.

If we judge from these estimates, textile workers were among the lower paid industrial workers in the nation. Their earnings were also well below the groups of white collar, governmental, and professional employees for which estimates are given, although the very low pay of school teachers, perhaps reflecting their part-year employment, should be noted. It is possible, of course, that the Douglas estimates for textile workers are lower than for some other industries because textiles were relatively more concentrated in the lower paying South. Even so, if we chose textile workers as a basis for assessing the annual earnings of industrial workers more generally, table 8.6 suggests that the result will be to underestimate the earnings of industrial workers as a whole. In other words, to the degree the data collection is representative of industrial workers, it is skewed toward lower income groups.

We will also recall from table 8.2 and elsewhere above that the annual earnings of textile workers included in the data appear noticeably higher than the estimated average earnings for the same groups given by Douglas. In fact the median and mean annual earnings of husbands calculated from the data collection are both approximately $396 as compared to the Douglas' estimates of $302 for cotton textile workers and $345 for those employed in manufacturing woolen and worsted goods.

Once again, we know that the data are not fully comparable. The Douglas estimates are confined to wage earners and exclude salaried employees in the industry; our source collection includes supervisors, some of whom were probably salaried. Recalculation excluding supervisors, however, reduces the medians and averages only slightly and by no means to the levels of the Douglas estimates.

A larger source of incomparability is that the Douglas estimates are for all employed textile workers of whatever age and sex. Calculations of earnings based on the data collection reflect only those of adult male workers who were presumably more highly paid than female and adolescent laborers. But even allowing for these incomparabilities, the impression remains that wage earners in textiles were among the lower paid industrial workers in the nation.

A second series of income estimates tends to confirm this general impression. By dividing estimated personal income for the nation and each state by total population, this series provides estimates of per capita income. For these purposes personal income is defined as income received by persons from all sources including wages, salaries, rents, interest, dividends, and the like. On this basis, per capita personal income is estimated at \$175 for 1880 and \$203 for 1900. No estimates are provided for 1890. However, we can estimate per capita personal income for 1890 by interpolation as \$189 if, that is, we assume that the rate of change in income levels was constant across the years from 1880 through 1900. We should stress that these estimates are for all occupations—farmers and farm laborers, business proprietors, professionals, and so on—as well as industrial workers.[3]

For purposes of comparability, we can estimate per capita income among

Table 8.6
Douglas Estimates of National Average Annual Earnings of Employed Wage Earners and Salaried Workers in Selected Industries and Areas of Employment, 1890*

Wage Earners

All Manufacturing	\$439
Clothing Industry	362
Agricultural Implements	534
Electrical Machinery	549
Furniture Manufacturing	464
Cigar and Cigarette Manufacturing	437
Beer and Soft Drink Manufacturing	630
Steam Railway	560
Street Railways (Street Cars)	557
Leather Goods Manufacturing	481
Stone, Clay and Glass Goods	433
Bituminous Coal Mining	406
Cotton Textiles	302
Woolen and Worsted Goods	345

Salaried Employees and Professionals

Salaried Employees In Manufacturing	872
Clerks on Railroads	635
Government Employees in Washington, D.C.(1892)	1026
All Clerical	848
Postal Employees	878
School Teachers	256
Methodist and Congregational Ministers	794

*Source: Paul H. Douglas, *Real Wages in the United States, 1890-1896* (Boston and New York: Houghton Mifflin Company, 1930), passim.

the textile workers and their families included in the data collections by dividing the total income received by all families by the total number of persons, in all families, excluding individuals in families with income from boarders. On this basis per capita income among the families appears as approximately $120. Once again, the data are consistent with the view that textile workers ranked in the lower, but probably not the lowest, income segments of the nation.

The characteristics of family living conditions that we observed in earlier chapters are at least compatible with this general conclusion. We may not be surprised to find that only about ten percent of the textile workers owned their homes. According to the Census of 1900, the first Census that collected data on home ownership, some 35 percent of the total nonfarm population of the nation owned their homes. The percentage of home owners was probably not greatly different ten years earlier. The smaller percentage of home owners among textile workers than among the nonfarm population more generally suggests, again, that textile workers were among the lower income segments of the national population. Our impression of marginal to inadequate clothing and food budgets on the part of many textile workers and their families that we gained in chapters 6 and 7 further reinforces the conclusion.

This brings us to the final question posed at the beginning of this section: can we draw any inferences on the basis of the data collection that are likely to be applicable to larger population groups almost regardless of the representative or nonrepresentative character of the data collection? At least in the case of family living conditions, the answer is yes, but with qualifications. The data provide information bearing upon a relatively wide range of annual earnings and per capita income. Even excluding the extremes of very high and very low income that included only a relatively small number of families, the income range represented by the data collection remains broad and, it is likely, extends into the middle ranges of income in the United States of the time.

It is plausible to conclude, in other words, that the sample underlying the data collection provides a basis for a useful and reasonably valid view of the kinds of living conditions that could be supported at the time at given levels of income in given areas of the nation. Problems such as the limitations of information on food and clothing prices and the unmeasured factor of home production have been noted above, but these do not concern the adequacy or inadequacy of the sample.

CONCLUSIONS

We cannot provide completely firm or categorical answers to questions concerning the representative quality of our source collection or the kinds of inferences it will or will not support. To explore these questions further would involve a research effort much beyond our present purposes, and even with such an extensive effort our answers would remain imperfect. We can, however, reach several reasonably firm conclusions concerning questions of this sort and the utility of our findings for an understanding of the society and economy of the United States at the close of the nineteenth century.

The source collection clearly does not provide a means to assess in any direct sense the income, living conditions, familial, or other characteristics of the wealthy or well-to-do, and it probably provides only limited suggestions of the living standards of the farm population. On the other hand, we will not go far wrong if we conclude that our "sample" of families is reasonably representative of urban industrial working class families of the time.

It is at least highly likely, then, that we have gained a reasonably accurate view of life among industrial workers and their families. Our sample is probably skewed toward lower income workers, and the view of living conditions is probably somewhat darker than was actually the case. On the other hand, ours is not a sample of the "poorest of the poor." It is not, in other words, a sample of the slum population of New York City so tellingly described by Jacob A. Riis in *How the Other Half Lives*.[4]

In these terms, we would be justified in concluding that the view we have gained of family structure and of variations in family size and practices from one regional and nationality group to the other is reasonably accurate. Similarly, the conclusion that the industrial working class tended to live in highly crowded conditions and was poorly dressed, certainly by modern standards, would also be reasonably justified.

If our further research into family diets led us to conclude that many of the families of *textile* workers were malnourished or were prey to dietary disorders and maladies, we could also conclude that many of the families of *industrial* workers at the time were also malnourished and suffered the same dietary disorders. All of this suggests, in short, that we have gained a detailed and reasonably accurate view of the industrial working class of the late nineteenth century.

TO THE READER

In this chapter we devoted considerable attention to the association between national background on the one hand, and variations in earnings on the other, and to attempting to decide whether we should interpret this association as reflecting a causal relationship. In other words, did differences in national background cause differences in earnings? It will be clear that the problem we face in this connection is an example of a more general problem. The problem is that the notion of causation is a theoretical concept which cannot be addressed solely on the basis of empirical data. The only way available to us to justify inferring causation is to rule out other factors that might be the source of observed associations.

In the present case, the only way we could proceed was to attempt to rule out other factors that might have been the actual source of the observed association between national background and variations in earnings. To this end we attempted to rule out region of residence and employment and occupation as possible sources of the observed association between national origins and earnings differentials. It will also be clear that this is a never-ending process. We can always think of other factors that may have been the actual cause of an observed association. In the case of the association between national origins and variations in earnings, two such possible additional factors will have already come mind.

One of these is age. We can certainly ponder whether the tendency of Northern native-stock workers to be younger than foreign-stock workers, observed in chapter 4, really rules out the possibility that the higher earnings of some native-stock workers were due to their greater age and experience. The mean age of native-stock textile workers was lower than that of other groups in the North, but the age range of the native stock was quite broad—from twenty to seventy-three. The number of supervisors and foremen, moreover, was quite small. Hence it is possible that the native-stock supervisors and foremen tended to be older workers who had gained experience and seniority and worked their way up through the years. In these terms age might prove to be a factor accounting for the higher earnings of the native stock.

The second factor is the specific industry of employment. This and preceding chapters have, in effect, assumed that textile manufacturing was a single industry. In fact, the industry had a number of components, two of which (cotton and woolens) are represented in the data collection. Table 8.6 also suggests that wages and earnings may have been lower in cotton textiles than in woolens.

We can readily imagine plausible reasons for such differences. Woolen textile manufacturing tended to be concentrated in the North while cotton textiles were manufactured everywhere. It might be assumed, therefore, that the competition of cheaper cotton textiles produced in the lower-paying South tended to depress wages in the cotton industry in the North. In the absence of Southern competition, wages in the woolen textile industry tended to be higher, or at least so the argument would run. Of course, we must remember that the average earnings given in table 8.6 reflect all regions—in the case of cotton textiles, the lower wages of the South as well as the higher wages of the North.

To address the second of these two possible factors first, table 8.7 displays the median annual earnings of cotton and woolen textile workers for the six Northern nationality groups used in earlier tables. Here again, the table treats the New England and Middle Atlantic states separately. As we can see, woolen textile workers in the Middle Atlantic states appear to have had higher earnings than their counterparts in the New England states. On the other hand, regional differences in the earnings of cotton textile workers are much more ambiguous. In general, however, the table gives no real support for the view that workers in woolen textiles were consistently more highly paid than workers in cotton textiles. Similarly, the table does not support the possibility that foreign-stock workers tended to have lower earnings because they were concentrated in a lower-paying segment of the textile industry.

We address the second possibility—that the higher earnings of native-stock workers were due to differences in age—in table 8.8. The general

Table 8.7
Median Earning of Cotton and Woolen Textile Workers by Regional and Nationality Groups

	Cotton		Wool	
	New England	Mid-Atlantic	New England	Mid-Atlantic
Northern Native Stock	$469.00	$485.00	$460.50	$505.00
Northern French Canadian	358.10	**	**	**
Northern Canadian	320.10	**	416.00*	**
Northern British	434.10	447.40	432.00	507.50
Northern Irish	387.00	323.00	370.00	384.50
Northern Continental European	390.00	353.00	350.00	443.00

* Twenty-five or fewer cases.
** Ten or fewer cases.

hypothesis is that higher-paid workers and workers employed in higher-paid occupational categories tended to be older than workers employed in lower-paying occupational categories. It will be recognized that this general hypothesis is related to the "family life cycle" hypothesis formulated in chapter 6 as a possible explanation of differences in family per capita income.

To address these and related hypotheses, table 8.8 gives the median ages for each occupational category for the eight regional and nationality groups used in earlier chapters. The reader can decide whether the table provides support for any hypotheses bearing upon the relationship between age and higher earnings or employment in higher-paid occupations. To phrase the question more precisely for present purposes, does the table support or refute the hypothesis that the association between nationality and levels of earnings observed in this and other chapters was really the product of differences in age between the several groups?

Whatever we make of these matters, one age difference reflected in the table is particularly striking: the tendency of common laborers to be older than workers in more highly paid employment categories. That difference appears most pronounced and consistent in the case of the Northern foreign-stock workers and among the native stock in the Border and Southern states and noticeably less pronounced and consistent among the Northern

Table 8.8
Median Age of Textile Workers by
Regional and Nationality Group and Occupational Category

	Supervisors	Foremen	Skilled Laborers	Semi-Skilled Laborers	Common Laborers
Northern Native Stock	39.3	33.9	36.4	32.1	38.2
Northern French Canadian	**	31.8*	34.0	35.3	43.0
Northern Canadian	**	**	34.5*	35.5	42.8
Northern British	42.0	34.5	41.1	38.7	45.5
Northern Irish	43.0*	40.5*	43.5	38.2	48.0
Northern Continental Europe	**	34.5*	41.1	35.3	47.7
Border State Native Stock	44.0*	36.5*	37.3	30.5	47.3
Southern Native Stock	35.0*	33.0	35.6	32.3	45.3

* Twenty-five cases or fewer
** Ten cases or fewer

native stock. The greater age of common laborers suggested by the data collection is compatible with at least two explanations, which are not mutually exclusive. In considering these explanations and pondering means to further test them, discussions in chapters 4 and 6 should be kept in mind.

One possible explanation is, of course, that many workers entered the labor force as common laborers and remained in that category through all or most of their employment history. For many workers, in other words, there was little or no occupational mobility. We might take the fact that this pattern was particularly pronounced among some groups, and less pronounced among the Northern native stock, as an indication of the greater disadvantages suffered by some nationality and regional groups.

A second possibility concerns the disadvantages of age itself or, perhaps, the presence of "age discrimination." Then, as in some degree today, younger workers tended to be valued more highly and to compete more successfully for higher-paying jobs than older workers. Indeed, so this argument would run, as workers aged they tended to be gradually shuffled to lower-paying and more menial occupations. Thus the common laborer occupation tended to be disproportionately populated by older workers. It will also be clear that these two explanations do not rule each other out. Both processes could have operated simultaneously.

NOTES

CHAPTER 1

1. *Sixth Annual Report of the Commissioner of Labor, 1890* (Washington: Government Printing Office, 1891), 688–90.

2. The index values are given in Bureau of the Census, *Historical Statistics of the United States from Colonial Times to 1970* (Washington, D.C.: Government Printing Office, 1975), and for more recent years in the annual issues of Bureau of the Census, *The Statistical Abstract of the United States* (Washington, D.C.: Government Printing Office).

CHAPTER 5

1. The use of the word "expected" above requires additional comment. If the relationship in figure 5.1 was perfect ($r = 1$)—if, in other words, only family income affected the percentage of income spent on necessities—then the expected value of Y for any given family would be the same as the actual percentage of income spent on necessities by that family. Since the correlation is not perfect, the expected value of Y departs from the actual value. Put differently, the equation does not predict the actual value of Y perfectly, and the departure of the expected value of Y in a given case from its actual value is a reflection of the error in the prediction. Thus the quation could be rewritten as:

$$Y = a + bX + e$$

where e is an error term expressing the deviation of the expected values of Y from the actual values. Alternatively the equation might be written as:

$$\hat{Y} = a + bX$$

where $\hat{Y}$ (sometimes referred to as Y hat) indicates the expected value of Y. It should be recognized that the procedure described here assumes a linear relationship between the variables of concern. That is, it assumes that the relationship between the variables can be meaningfully described in terms of a straight line. As will be seen at a later point, the relationship between two variables cannot always be meaningfully described in terms of a straight line.

CHAPTER 6

1. William Burton Hartley, "Estimation of the Incidence of Poverty in the United States," Unpublished Doctoral Dissertation, University of Wisconsin, 1969, pp. 46–51 and 484–486.

CHAPTER 7

1. U.S. Congress. Senate. Committee on Finance. "Retail Prices and Wages" (Govt. Printing Office: Washington, D.C., 1892).

CHAPTER 8

1. Washington, D.C.: Government Printing Office, 1918.
2. Boston and New York: Houghton Mifflin, 1930.
3. See Everett S. Lee. Ann Ratner Miller, Carol P. Brainerd and Richard A. Easterlin, *Population and Economic Growth, United States, 1980–1950*, vol. 1, *Methodological Considerations and Reference Tables* (Philadelphia: American Philosophical Society, 1975), p. 753.
4. New York: Scribner and Sons, 1890.

SUGGESTIONS FOR FURTHER READING

There is an abundance of rich source material which will enhance and complement this volume. Cited below are works which we have found to be particularly useful. The first is a set of current government publications. Especially valuable are recent volumes from the series entitled the *Statistical Abstract of the United States* (U.S. Bureau of the Census: Washington, D.C.) These provide a wealth of information on contemporary household characteristics as well as data on health, nutrition, income, expenditures, and prices in the present period which are invaluable for comparative purposes. As indicated in the text, the *Statistical Abstract of the United States* for 1980 in particular provides useful data on the distribution of expenditures for personal consumption. Similarly, the U.S. Bureau of the Census's *Historical Statistics of the United States from Colonial Time to 1970* (Washington, D.C.: Government Printing Office, 1975) includes numerous social and economic data series, many of which extend back into the nineteenth century. These volumes should be readily available in the reference section or government publications department of most academic libraries.

The *1897 Sears and Roebuck Catalog* (edited by Fred L. Israel) (New York: Chelsea House Publishers, 1968) and the *Montgomery Ward & Co. Catalogue and Buyers Guide*, No. 57, Spring and Summer, 1895, unabridged reprint by Maurice Emmett, (New York: Dover Publishers, Inc., 1969) offer valuable information on the availability and prices of a wide range of items such as clothing and household goods. In addition, many city newspapers in the late 1880s regularly included advertisements for clothing, fabrics, furniture, entertainment, and housing. Readers may also want to consult local newspapers, if available, for similar information.

Excellent textual material, offering insights into the living conditions of Americans in the late-nineteenth and early-twentieth centuries, is also available. Margaret Byington's *Homestead: The Households of Milltown* (Pittsburgh: The University of

Pittsburgh Press, 1974) [originally published in 1910] is a classic sociological study of the living conditions of steel workers in the early twentieth century; it provides a wealth of data on work, wages, budgets, and the costs of living of steel workers. Readers will find the data in this volume useful for making comparisons with the standard of living of textile workers described in this book. Jacob A. Riis's *How the Other Half Lives: Studies Among the Tenements of New York* (New York: Dover Publications, Inc., 1971) [originally published in 1890] includes numerous firsthand observations, photographs, and drawings of life and living conditions among the poor of New York City in the late nineteenth century. In contrast to Riis, Ethel Spencer's *The Spencers of Amberson Avenue: A Turn of the Century Memoir*, edited by Michael P. Weber and Peter N. Stearns (Pittsburgh: The University of Pittsburgh Press, 1983) is the recollection of a professor of English written in the late 1950s of growing up in a middle- or upper-middle-class family in Pittsburgh at the turn of the century.

Jane Addams' *Twenty Years at Hall House* (New York: MacMillan, 1935 and David M. Katzman and William M. Tuttle, Jr., eds. *Plain Folk* (Urbana: University of Illinois Press, 1982) also offer insights into living conditions of Americans at the turn of the century. Tamara K. Hareven's and Randolph Langenback's *Amoskeag: Life and Work in an American Factory City* (New York: Pantheon Books, 1978) is an oral history of textile workers at the turn of the century. Also valuable is Dorothy Richardson's *The Story of a Working Girl*, originally published in 1905 and reprinted in William O'Neill, ed. *Women at Work* (New York: Quadrangle/New Times Book Company, 1972). This work dramatizes the living conditions and experiences of a New York girl at the turn of the century.

In addition to this source material, the reader is directed to Joseph W. Barnes's "How to Raise a Family on $500 a Year," *American Heritage*, 33 (December 1981): 91–95. This essay describes an exhibit at the 1893 Columbian Exhibition, which included a life-size house complete with experimental family. The project was chiefly the work of Katherine Bement Davis, a nutritionist from Rochester, New York. Convinced that the application of sound natural science could help solve social and economic problems, Davis's goal in putting together the exhibit was to educate Americans in terms of efficient household management and to indicate how a family of four could live on an annual income of $500.

INDEX